MAN WITH A DREAM

THE STORY OF SAINT JOHN BOSCO

by

PETER M. RINALDI, S.D.B.

SALESIANA PUBLISHERS
New Rochelle, New York

To the parishioners of Corpus Christi Church,
Port Chester, N.Y.

God's people and my people. I count it a singular
grace and a joy to have ministered to them
for twenty-nine unforgettable years.

IMPRIMI POTEST:
   Very Rev. Salvatore Isgro, S.D.B.
   Provincial

First Printing
   January 1978

Second Printing
   July 1978

Third Printing
   July 1981

Fourth Printing
   April 1997

Cover design: Ariana Grabec
Printed in the United States of America

CONTENTS

FOREWARD

MAN WITH A DREAM is the story of St. John Bosco—
Don Bosco, as he was and still is popularly known—a tower-
ing figure during one of the most critical periods in the history of the Catholic Church. Founder of the Salesian Order,
whose members number close to forty thousand, he was
the trusted friend of popes, kings, statesmen and literati,
and played no small part in the affairs of both Church and
State in 19th century Italy.

But it was his consuming interest in the young, the
poorest and most neglected among them, that won for him
the admiration of the world. From his compassionate love
for them came countless homelike establishments and
a uniquely successful system of education based on reason,
religion and kindness. "Don Bosco, you have done wonders!"
Pope Leo XIII told him. "You yourself do not realize the
extent of your mission, and the good it will bring to the
world."

From the day he was born in a humble cottage in
Piedmont, Italy, to the day on which two hundred thousand persons lined Turin's boulevards to mourn at his funeral, the life of Don Bosco unfolds with more drama and color
than any historical novel.

Drama and color are found on every page of this book.
Anecdotes, culled from the 20-volume Biographical Memoirs
of Don Bosco and from the testimony of persons who

knew the Saint, are woven by the author into a delightful portrait of this extraordinary priest, who charmed youngsters and awed the great, and whose zestful, buoyant personality is one of the richest and most colorful in the history of the Church.

It is not only Don Bosco who comes to life in these pages, but many of the interesting people who moved around him: his extraordinary mother for one, and, too, some of the youngsters he befriended, as well as the men and women who either helped or opposed him. It is an immensely readable story in which every anecdote is historical, and every dialogue and quotation authentic, if not always literal.

The author gives grateful acknowledgement to the Very Reverend Salvatore Isgro, SDB, Provincial Superior of the Salesian Society, Eastern Province, New Rochelle, N.Y., without whose encouragement this work would not have been undertaken; and to Miss Marie Prochilo, Port Chester, N.Y., without whose assistance it would not have been brought to completion.

CHAPTER I

WHAT WILL THIS CHILD BE?

"A Dream I Had. . ."

A dream I had when I was nine years old left an indelible impression on my mind. I dreamt I was in a large field, not far from home, with a crowd of boys, most of whom were playing, while some were at their worst behavior, as was evidenced by their foul language. I went right up to them and began to rough them up with my fist and harsh words, when suddenly a man appeared, clad in a dazzling white robe, his bearing noble and majestic, his face so bright, I could hardly bear to look at him. He called me by name and told me to take charge of those boys, adding: "You will never make them your friends by treating them that way. Be kind and gentle with them. Come now, show them how they can mend their ways and become decent boys."

I was so awed and frightened that all I could do was stammer something about being a poor ignorant boy, quite unable to lecture anyone, let alone those boys. I noticed, in the meantime, that they all had left their games and had quietly gathered around the mysterious man. I then spoke to him again; and, not quite knowing what I was saying, I ventured to say to him, "Who are you to tell me to do such impossible things?"

"What seems impossible to you now," he answered, "you will be able to do later through obedience and study."

1

"But how can I ever hope to be able to study and learn about those things?"

"I will give you a guide, who can instruct you as no one else can."

"But who are you to speak to me that way?"

"You know my mother. You greet her three times a day, the way your mother taught you."

"My mother always tells me not to have anything to do with strangers, unless I ask her permission. Tell me your name."

Suddenly I saw a stately lady at his side, wearing a beautiful mantle, all studded with gems that shone like stars. Seeing how hopelessly confused I was, she bade me come close to her, and taking my hand, "Look," she said. The boys had all vanished, and in their place were now all sorts of animals: goats, dogs, wild cats, bears. . . . "This will be your field of action," the lady continued, "but first you must grow up to be humble, strong and sturdy. The change you will now see in these animals, you will then bring about in my children."

I looked again, and all those wild beasts were suddenly changed into lambs, bleating and playfully skipping all around us. It was all too much for me, and I started to cry while I kept begging the lady to tell me what all this meant. She gently placed her hand on my head, "Someday, in due time," she said, smiling, "you will understand everything." It was at this point that I awoke and realized that it was all a dream.

When in the morning I told my two brothers about my dream, they both had a good laugh. Joseph suggested that I would probably become a shepherd and tend "not just sheep, but cows, goats, and all sorts of animals."

"You may well end up by becoming the leader of a gang of bandits," Anthony snickered. Mother said quietly, "Who knows, Johnny, you might even become a priest." Grandmother, who though illiterate was wiser than all of us, said resolutely, "We shouldn't pay the slightest attention to dreams."

I was quite sure she was right, but that dream kept haunting me for the rest of my life.

"Your Father is Dead!"

John, our young dreamer, was born on August 16, 1815, in Becchi, a tiny hamlet near Turin in Piedmont, Italy. His father, Francis Bosco, died when John was barely two years old.

"Margaret," he told his wife in a whisper as he lay dying, "I know you will do your best with the children. Take care of our little John in a special way." Sobbing, she knelt in prayer by his bed, the three children near her, until she realized Francis had stopped breathing. She then drew the sheet over his face, and turning to the youngsters, "Come now," she told them calmly, "we must leave." But John, his eyes fixed on the bed, would not move.

"We must go, Johnny. Come with me." And she gently led the child away.

"I want papa to come with us, Mommy!"

"My poor child, your father is dead!"

It was early summer, 1817. Francis Bosco's family was left to face a future that was far from promising. Of the children, Anthony, a son by Francis' previous marriage, was then eleven, a surly, difficult boy; Joseph was five, and John nearly two. And there was Francis' mother, a frail old woman, partly paralyzed and in need of constant care.

Those were difficult times for Piedmont, first overrun by the armies of Napoleon and later plagued by constant inroads of mercenaries, who literally laid the countryside to waste. In spite of all that, the young widow was grateful. "It's going to be a bit harder without your father," she told the family after the funeral, "but we'll manage with God's help. Our home is not much, but at least we have a roof over our heads. Let us be thankful, too, that we have a bit of land and a cow, things other people do not have." To the tearful youngsters and the distraught mother-in-law, what mattered most was that they had her, Margaret Occhiena Bosco, who had a man's strength and the most gentle and loving heart God ever bestowed on a woman.

"What Now, Johnny?"

John grew sprightly, vigorous, and full of mischief. "Too much quick-silver in his veins," Grandma Bosco would often say about her favorite grandson.

He was seven years old when one day, during his mother's absence, balancing himself precariously on a high stool, he tried to reach for something in the cupboard. He only succeeded in toppling a large crock of oil which came tumbling down with a crash, spilling the precious content all over the kitchen floor. "What will Mother say?" was his first thought as he ran to grab a broom which only made a worse mess on Margaret's spotless brick floor.

To forestall trouble, there was only one thing to do. He went to the yard, snipped a branch from the willow tree and proceeded to strip off its leaves as he sat by the kitchen door, waiting for his mother. He soon spotted her coming up the road; and, holding the whip behind his back, ran to meet her.

"Hello, Johnny. Have you been a good boy?"

John produced the whip and a face that said, "I am at your mercy."

"What now? What have you done?"

Out came a sad story in one breath, ending with: "This time I really deserve a whipping, Mother." But how could Margaret resist the mischievous look on the boy's face? She ruffled his curls, and "Come along," she said. "Let's get home fast so we can clean up the mess before Grandma sees it."

"Ghosts," You Say?

It was known around Becchi that John was a plucky little fellow with a spirit and courage far beyond his age. He was hardly nine when he had his first successful bout with "ghosts."

The family was visiting at the farm of Margaret's parents in Capriglio when on the first evening someone who had gone to the bedrooms upstairs quickly came down to tell the assembled family that mysterious noises were coming from the attic.

Margaret's two brothers went up to the bedrooms; but

were soon back, a bit shaken. "It is true. There are noises coming from the attic—and very peculiar ones, too. They sound like the shuffling and stamping of feet, and occasionally as if someone were hitting the floor with a stick. But what's strange is that the noises actually seem to follow you from room to room." The children were frightened, and the adults impressed.

"Why not go to see what goes on in the attic?" John volunteered.

"Are you out of your mind?" Grandma Occhiena replied. "Not you, nor anyone else! Certainly not tonight in the dark. . ." Even Margaret was not too sure John was being sensible.

"But something has to be done," John pleaded. "Who's coming with me?" He snatched one of the lamps from the table and started up the stairway leading to the attic. Some of the men followed him, ashamed that a mere child should beat them to the game.

What met their eyes, in the flickering light of the lamp, was indeed a strange thing. A huge, round sieve—the kind used for cornflour—was actually moving on the floor. "Get back, Johnny, get back! Don't go near it!. . .It's a ghost moving it; it's the devil!" But John, stepping forward, lifted the sieve; and out came the "ghost," a great big rooster, half-blinded by the light, his feathers ruffled, looking more dead than alive. John grabbed it, held it up, and laughing: "Here is the ghost! Here is the devil!" he shouted.

Downstairs they were all relieved, and wondered how the rooster had gotten itself into that fix. Grandpa Occhiena explained it easily. The bird had found its way to the attic and began to peck at whatever remnant of corn was in the sieve which someone had placed upright against the wall. The sieve fell on the rooster, which was then trying might and main to free itself from the trap. John got more back-slapping than he cared to receive, and everyone applauded when he suggested the "ghost" be served for dinner on the following day.

"You Are Forever in Trouble. . ."

Margaret was washing her nine-year old's face, streaked with mud and blood.

"You are forever in trouble, Johnny. Yesterday it was your leg; now it's your head. What next? Can't you keep away from those rowdies?"

"But, Mom, when I am with them, they behave. . . ."

"One wouldn't think so by looking at you. I forbid you to go out with them again. They are too rough. . . ."

"You don't believe me, Mom, but they really do behave when I am with them." The boy looked at his mother pleadingly.

"What am I going to do with you, Johnny?" And in the smile she gave him were her unspoken words: "All right, Johnny, but please be careful!. . ."

"Take My Bread."

Young John did his share of work on the Becchi farm. One of his chores was to look after the family cow and to take it to pasture in the nearby fields. One day he met a boy of his age, Secondo Matta, who was engaged in the same task. Thin, ragged and barefooted, Secondo was a study in contrast to John whose family was certainly as poor as Secondo's, but whose mother kept him always neatly dressed and well-fed.

John noticed the poor quality of Secondo's bread—coarse, stale and tasteless—while his own was fragrant, light, and fresh from Margaret's oven: "Becchi's tastiest bread," people used to say.

"How about a taste of your bread?" he asked Secondo one morning, adding, "You can have some of mine." It went further than just a taste, since, from that day on, John would exchange his entire loaf with Secondo.

"But, John, why do you exchange your bread for mine when yours is so much better?" Secondo wanted to know.

"It's just that I like yours a lot more, Secondo."

It didn't make sense to Secondo, but then there were many other things about Margaret's son people wondered about.

"He Will Have the Whole World Talking!"

"We'll meet at Margaret's home tonight. Her Johnny will read and perform again." The word spread quickly around Becchi.

Standing on a stool so all could hear and see him, John, barely in his teens, would read for hours on end during the long winter nights. Often he would tell stories, interspersing them with jokes and even sleight-of-hand tricks. In the midst of it all, he would suddenly stop, pull out the rosary beads from his pocket, and: "We'll now offer a decade," he would say with a smile that no one could resist.

In the summer his entertainment took on a different form. He had developed an uncanny ability to do tricks, gymnastics and acrobatic stunts, by dint of observing and imitating circus performers at country fairs. He usually performed Sunday afternoons in the field in front of his cottage, but was often invited by neighboring peasants to present his act in haylofts and barns. Here, too, at the most tense moment, when his audience stood spell-bound, "How about the Rosary, people?" or, "Here is a brief summary of a sermon I once heard," he would say quietly. And if a few of the spectators wandered off, "The best is yet to come," he would shout. "Join us now or stay away altogether."

Margaret, gazing from her cottage or standing among the crowd, often wondered about her youngster who mesmerized those simple country folks by juggling eggs, pulling a rabbit out of a hat, plucking a silver coin from a nose or ear, and gingerly walking a tightrope. She wondered, too, how her son could so effortlessly turn those people's thoughts to God and make them pray so well. One day, after one such performance, she asked her neighbor Caterina Agagliati, "Tell me, Caterina, what do you make of my Johnny? What do you think he will be?"

Signora Agagliati spoke her native Piedmontese with unusual solemnity this time. "That boy," she said, "will have the whole world talking some day."

CHAPTER II

MAMA MARGARET

"I Believe He Really Loved Me."

There was not the slightest doubt in the neighbors' minds that Francis Bosco's young and attractive widow was a woman to be reckoned with. But would she be up to the task confronting her? By the end of 1817, the year of her husband's death, everyone at Becchi knew that she was.

Margaret was determined to keep the family together and to run the household just as if Francis were still with them. The care of the children and of her sickly mother-in-law came first on her busy schedule, although she had to be out in the fields, too. She soon proved to herself and to all concerned that she could work just like a man. There was not a thing she could not do, no matter how hard, and do it well.

But the home was where her heart was. "Margaret lives only for her children," people would say when they saw her trudging up the hill to the parish church, her children happily skipping around her. They knew the young widow had had several attractive offers to marry and had turned them down with a shrug and a smile. "I have my children and my mother-in-law to care for. We are a happy family, and I have my health and my two strong arms. Why upset the applecart?"

Years later, Margaret enlarged on the motive that had

11

made her decide not to marry again. "In one instance," she confided to a friend, "I nearly did it. He was very kind and considerate; a man of means, too; and I believe he really loved me. Yet I was firmly convinced that God had already given me a wonderful husband for a purpose. That same God took my Francis away. I had a duty to fulfill, since my husband, when dying, had entrusted the three boys to me in a very special manner. There really never was any other alternative. My path was clearly marked for me. All I had to do was to follow the road signs ahead, step by step, I had to become both mother and father, all in one.

"Look, Mom; Isn't It Beautiful?"

There are any number of anecdotes that bring out the innate wisdom, faith and strength of Margaret Occhiena Bosco.

One evening, Joseph and John were watching the sun setting behind the Alps in a blaze of colorful lights.

"Look, Mom; isn't it beautiful?"

"The Lord has done it all, my children. How great He must be!"

Late one night, when it was nearly time for bed, the two youngsters, their arms on the sill of the open window, kept looking at the myriad stars twinkling away in an ocean of blackness.

"They are beautiful, Mom!"

"And shouldn't they be, my sons, since it is the Lord himself who put them there? If this side of heaven is so lovely, what must the other side be?"

Billowing clouds suddenly darkened the sky on a hot summer day. Rain was pouring down in sheets. The youngsters ran to Margaret and shivered with fear when lightning and thunder struck.

"I am scared, Mom!. . . ."

"How mighty the Lord is!. . .But we never need fear if we are good. . ."

"I Thought You Weren't Thirsty."

There was nothing angelic about Joseph's or John's make-up, unless it was their cherubic faces under heads of brown curls. One hot summer afternoon, the two brothers came running into the kitchen. "Mama, a drink of water, please!"

Margaret dipped her copper ladle into an earthenware jug of water and presented it first to Joseph, the older of the two. John resented the preference and when, in turn, his mother raised the ladle to his lips, he sulkily refused to drink. Not a word from Margaret, who simply put the ladle back into the jug and resumed her work. The jealous little rascal needed a lesson.

A few minutes later, "Mama. . ." Her four-year old bambino was tugging at her skirt.

"What now, Johnny?"

"A drink, please, Mama. . ."

"I thought you weren't thirsty!"

"I am sorry. . . ."

"Now that's what I like to hear, son," and a smiling Margaret ran to fetch her cherub a drink of cold water.

"My Poor Blackbird!"

There were hardly any feathers on the hapless little blackbird John found on the ground, shivering wet, after an early summer thundershower. He took it home, nursed it back to health, and watched it grow, its shining dark plumage a joy to the touch. They became inseparable companions. They ate together, whistled and warbled together, the bird responding to John's call from every corner of the house.

One morning there was no answer to the soft whistle with which John always greeted his feathered friend from his bedroom at dawn. He ran to the makeshift cage he had made for it and had hung near the kitchen window; he found it on the floor in shambles, and the bird a mess of bloodied feathers. Nero, the family tomcat, had done his savage deed only too well.

The boy was heartbroken. "My poor blackbird!. . ." he kept repeating between sobs. Nothing Margaret said could bring a measure of comfort to him. Irked by all that crying, one day she told him bluntly: "Aren't you carrying this too far, Johnny? So many tears over such a tiny loss? What would you do if I were to die?" Suddenly Johnny saw the light. He looked up amidst his tears, smiled, and threw his arms around her neck.

"I Would Rather See You Dead!"

They had all gone to Castelnuovo for Sunday Mass: Margaret and the two younger children together, while Anthony, as usual, had made it there with his friends. On the way back to Becchi, they ran into a group of men, most of them young, who seemed to be having the time of their life listening to the loud jokes of an older man. When the latter caught sight of the young widow, he raised his voice and launched into indecent remarks.

Margaret was appalled. She turned to him and, in no uncertain terms, let him have the tongue lashing she thought he deserved.

"At your age, how dare you use such language in front of these young people and my own children?"

"I only meant it as a joke, lady. . ."

"But you know that what you said is filthy wrong. Why did you say it?"

"Because we want to laugh a little. Nothing wrong with that, is there?"

"You can laugh your way to hell if you want, but you don't have to drag other people there with you. . ."

By the time she got through, the group melted away. To the children, who had never seen her so indignant, she then said with a broken voice: "I love you more than my life, but I would rather see you dead than know you will turn out to be like that monster."

"Do You Really Mean Those Words?"

As he grew, Anthony became the problem in the Bosco household. A bully, who could not get along with anyone, he was particularly hard on John and never missed a chance to tell him off.

One evening they were all at prayer by the fireplace. Mama Margaret, who was leading the Lord's Prayer, suddenly stopped. "One minute," she said, and turning to Anthony, "Tony, before you say 'forgive us our trespasses,' ask yourself if you really mean those words." She spoke calmly and deliberately.

"Why not?" Anthony answered, more surprised than defiant.

"Because," Margaret continued, "you have nothing but hatred in your heart, judging from the way you have been acting lately. Why don't you change, Tony? You know we love you. . ."

"I promise, Mother! I'll try. . ."

Margaret resumed the prayer. Suddenly she felt grateful. For months Anthony had not called her "Mother." Who knows? Maybe this time she had reached his heart.

"It's Your Big Day, Johnny!"

Father Sismondo was not easily persuaded. A man of few words, he even appeared slightly impatient with Margaret, who stood respectfully before him, with John at her side, a look of expectancy on her face.

"Why this hurry, Margaret?" John is not even eleven

years old. You know that children are not admitted to first Holy Communion until after their twelfth birthday."

"He knows his catechism, Father. He is. . ."

"I will think about it. In any case, he must attend religious instruction class. That means coming daily all the way from Becchi, all through Lent. . ."

"I won't mind at all, Father," John said eagerly.

The priest did not as much as look at the boy, and dismissed Margaret with a curt bow.

It was John who broke the silence as they left the parish house. "Father had nothing to say to me, Mom. . ."

"Priests are very busy, Johnny. They have lots of problems they must think about. You can hardly expect them to waste their time on a boy your age. . ."

A brief silence, and John spoke up again: "Mom, if I ever become a priest, I will have lots of time for children."

Margaret gently pressed the boy to her side, as she was wont to do whenever she couldn't think of the right word to say.

After a few catechism instructions, Father Sismondo sent for Margaret. "Your son is quite a lad," he told her. "Yes, a fine, bright boy. He knows his catechism perfectly. If you taught him, Margaret, you certainly did a good job. We will admit him to Holy Communion."

For days mother and son savored the joy of the event to come. Father Sismondo readily assented to Margaret's request to allow John to receive Holy Communion privately. "It is just as well," he said. "John is too young, and he would be out of place with the other youngsters." It was decided he would receive Holy Communion with Margaret and Joseph.

On the eventful morning, Margaret had John all to herself, fussing over the outfit she had made for him. Her words to him came easily. "This is your big day, Johnny. It is a great gift the Lord is about to make to you. But He expects a gift from you, too: your heart. Tell Him you want to belong to Him for the rest of your life. Tell Him to keep you good always."

"I will, Mom. And I will pray for you, too. . ."

CHAPTER III

THE LONG, HARD ROAD

"I'll Never Bother You Again."

It was a sight the good Becchi folks were not used to: Margaret's youngest son tending the cows in the pasture, with a book in his hands, absorbed in study. Some even poked fun at him in a pleasant sort of way. "John, what in the world are you aiming to become with your nose forever buried in those books?"

"Something good, I hope," he would answer with a smile.

At first, some of his young friends were annoyed with him. "Do you have to study all the time, Johnny? We need you for our games. We can't play without you."

"You forget I played with you yesterday. Now I have to study. I'll join you some other time."

One day, one of the older boys, impatient and determined, became somewhat rough with him, and even threatened to drag him away forcibly from his books. John's friends came to his rescue. "Leave him alone, Andy! He hasn't done anything to you, has he? What if he wants to study? Johnny wants to become a priest."

"Johnny, you a priest?" Bewilderment and awe were suddenly spread all over Andrew's face. "A priest, Johnny? I didn't know. I'll never bother you again," he muttered. "Never again!"

"It's What I Say!"

Margaret dreaded the thought of another quarrel. There had been too many unpleasant scenes since Anthony, her stepson, had turned twenty-one. He now wanted to be consulted on everything. "Remember, Margaret," he said once, "from now on, it's not what you think; it's what I say."

This time she was determined to make her point. Alone with him one evening after supper, she broached the subject to him.

"Tony," she said calmly, "Don't you think we could send Johnny to school this fall?"

"Send John to school, did you say? Is he really so special? There is work to be done on the farm, and I am not going to break my back so he can become a professor or something. . ."

Margaret pressed her point as gently as possible. "You know he wants to become a priest, Tony. Is it right to stand in his way?"

"Who's going to pay for his schooling?" he shouted and raged. "We don't have enough money to buy seed for next year's wheat crop, and you want to send him to school!"

He pounded on the table. "No, no, by God," he shouted, "No school for John or anyone else in this house!"

Margaret sighed. "There has to be another solution," she said, and with tears in her eyes, she left him to his ranting.

"It's the Only Way, Johnny!"

The solution, Margaret knew, was heart-rending. She postponed it for several weeks. "Johnny," she told him one day, "I have thought about it for a long time. Tony is impossible. There is only one way. Leave us for a while. Go to the Moglias at Moncucco. They are fine people. I know they can use someone like you."

She prepared a bundle of clothes and made sure his books were included. "It's only for a short while, Johnny. As you know, Tony is planning to get married. At least you'll have some peace at the Moglias. The work will be no harder than here, and they might even pay you."

It was a tearful parting for both, which left John little prepared for what was awaiting him at the Moglia farm. It was getting dark when he arrived at the sprawling farmhouse. The gruff voice of the tall, thin man he met by the barn was not very reassuring.

"And what, might I ask, brings you here at this late hour?"

"I am Johnny Bosco, Margaret's son, from Becchi. Are you Signor Moglia?"

"I am. But you are not telling me why you came here. . ."

John broke down as he told his story, and concluded: "Please, take me, Signor Moglia! I'll do anything, anything at all! You don't have to pay me. . ."

"You come at the wrong time, boy." The man's voice had softened. "We don't hire farmhands until spring. You better go back to Becchi."

It was at this point that Dorothy, Moglia's wife, who had

overheard the conversation from the barn, intervened. "Luigi, take the boy, if only for a few days. I feel terribly sorry for him, and besides, we know his mother."

John became the Moglias' favorite farmboy. For nearly two years his days were filled with work, and evenings saw him pour over his beloved books. When sleep finally overtook him, it was always with a prayer that his lifedream might some day come true.

"Leave It to Me."

"He is all heart," people used to say of Don Calosso. Indeed, no one could help but love Murialdo's elderly vicar. They turned to him more readily than they did to Don Sismondo, the cold and aloof pastor of Castelnuovo. John loved the good priest who, in turn, had taken a great interest in the boy.

"You do like to study, don't you, Johnny?" the priest had asked him once on a chance meeting.

"Oh, yes, Father! I want to become a priest like you!"

"Tell your mother to come to see me, Johnny."

Margaret poured out her heart to the priest. "Of course I want the boy to go to school, Father. But how can that ever be with Anthony against it? It's unbearable since Johnny came back from the Moglia farm. Oh, Father, if only something could be done!"

"I think it can, Margaret. Leave it to me. Beginning tomorrow, I want Johnny every afternoon at five o'clock. On rainy days, when he does not have to go out to work, he can come and stay all day."

John was ecstatic. A teacher all to himself! And Don Calosso, too! By Christmas that year, John had mastered most of the Latin grammar; by Easter, he was reading the classics with ease. "That Johnny is a prodigy! And an angel of a boy, too!" It was the way Don Calosso described him to Angelina, his old housekeeper, who nodded approvingly.

"And So Did Our Donkey!"

Anthony was soon back to his old game. "There is work to be done, and it is not done by studying Latin," he jeered one evening at the supper table.

"Johnny is doing his share," Margaret suggested. "After all, he is only fourteen."

"When I was his age I managed the farm alone. He is not earning the food he eats. I am sick of seeing books around the house. You don't need books to run a farm. What you need is a strong back and a will to work. I grew big and strong without the help of books!"

"So did the donkey in our stable," John remarked, making off as fast as his legs could carry him.

When on the following day the boy informed Don Calosso that things were as bad as ever at home, the good priest remained thoughtful for a few moments. "I tell you what, Johnny," he said suddenly. "Leave Becchi and come and stay with me. You'll help me with things around the church, and I will continue to assist you with your studies. Tell Mother not to worry from now on. I'll take care of you as long as I live, and even afterwards."

"If It's the Money You Want. . ."

A few months later, Don Calosso lay dying of a heart attack. John was shattered.

"The key, Johnny," the priest whispered to him shortly before he died. "Under my pillow. . .The money in the safe is all yours, for your schooling. Take it to your mother. No one need know about it. . ."

On the very day the priest expired, relatives, never before seen at the rectory, appeared on the scene. From the room where John was tearfully praying with a few people by Don Calosso's casket, he overheard them whisper.

"The boy must have the key," someone was saying. "Don Calosso probably left him whatever money he had. He loved him like a son. . ."

"Sorry," a more resolute voice was saying, "I am his nephew. The law is with me; that is, until a document proves otherwise."

John, his heart breaking, looked at Don Calosso's peaceful countenance and quietly left the room to face the priest's relatives.

"Here is the key," he said. "There are no documents. If it's the money you want, you may have it."

CHAPTER IV

TOWARD THE GOAL

One Step Closer

With Anthony married and finally out of the way, the thing to do was for John to enroll in the Castelnuovo school. He did, and for several weeks walked twice daily all of the twelve miles from Becchi to Castelnuovo and back, barefooted, carrying his shoes slung over his shoulder to save them from wearing.

"Johnny," Margaret said to him one day when the first snow flurries were beginning to fly under gray skies: "Johnny, it might be best if you stayed at Castelnuovo during the week. I talked to John Roberti, the tailor. He'll be glad to have you lodge at his home. All he wants is a weekly provision of eggs and vegetables, which I can easily supply. You might assist him with a bit of work around the shop, too..."

The lodging arrangement was ideal, but the school was not. John was a growing boy of sixteen among village children younger than he, in a typical one-room schoolhouse where a beleaguered teacher taught youngsters at different grade levels. He felt out of place. "I'm really wasting my time," he told his mother.

"Maybe Chieri is the answer," Margaret suggested.

"Chieri! Where the Seminary is!" John was thrilled. One step closer to the goal.

25

But then the nagging question again. "What about the money, Mother?" he asked anxiously.

"I have it all figured out, Johnny. You will board with Signora Lucia Matta, who will be satisfied with five liras a month plus the food I will supply. All she asks is that you occasionally tutor her son. Besides, cousin John Pianta will welcome your services at his restaurant, and that should help, too."

When word spread at Becchi that John was leaving for Chieri, people came to the Bosco cottage with items of clothing, and food: all kinds of cheese, salami, bread, bottles of wine, and beans piled up high on the kitchen table. "Use what you can, and turn the rest into money," they told John. "You'll need it! And good luck, Johnny! We'll miss you!"

For the peasant boy from Becchi, Chieri, though a small provincial town, was a marked improvement over Castelnuovo. Its beautiful churches and shops, its piazzas and quaint porticoed streets gave it a distinct atmosphere. it was mainly a student center where Jesuits, Dominicans, Franciscans and half dozen other religious orders had their schools and seminaries. Like John, most of the students roomed out, often working at odd jobs for their room and board.

Lucia Matta was more than happy to have John. A widow, she knew her son would now have a reliable friend and an excellent tutor. Cousin John Pianta, too, found John an ideal part-time waiter at his busy restaurant. John's days were filled with study and work. At school he became quite popular with his fellow students, both for his brilliant scholarship and for his congenial character and physical prowess. Still, there was something unique about this sturdy, pleasant-looking student.

"I saw him kneeling at the altar in the Cathedral one day," one of the students said. "He wasn't just praying; he was actually talking to someone. You should have seen his face! Like a saint!. . . You know, I sometimes wonder about John Bosco."

"The Happy Club"

They all knew John had a way with his schoolmates. "Let's form a club," he told a few of his teenage friends one day. "We'll call it 'The Happy Club.' " No fast rules, no dues. He set the program in a few simple words: To live our Christian faith and engage in all forms of wholesome, clean fun. John threw his net wide, but would have nothing to do with the irreligious, the indifferent, and the foul-mouthed.

The club was an instant success. On Sundays they met for Mass, followed by excursions to the surrounding countryside. Often they tramped the twelve miles to Turin to see the sights of the great city then in its heyday. Country fairs, very popular in Piedmont, were also occasions for exciting fun.

It was at one of these fairs that John provided his friends with a treat as unexpected as it was welcome. One of the fair's attractions was a greased pole surmounted with tempting prizes: cash, hams, salami, and bottles of the region's select wines. The pole was unusually high and greased to a spit-polish smoothness. Several youngsters tried their hands and legs in futile efforts to climb to the top.

"Come on, John! You can do it!. . ." The cry of one of the bystanders was taken up by a chorus of voices.

"I'll try it," John answered quietly. Gripping the pole firmly with his legs and feet as well as with his hands, which he occasionally wiped on his trousers, John inched his way to the top of the pole amidst the rousing cheers of his friends, thrilled as much by their leader's victory as by the prospect of a treat the mouth-watering prizes supplied. They all agreed this was one of the Happy Club's most memorable events.

"I'll Challenge You. . ."

There were other occasions on which John had to exert himself considerably in order to retain his influence on his club. One Sunday, just as he was preparing to lead his friends to Mass, an acrobat appeared on the square in front of the church, loudly proclaiming the marvels of his performance. John knew that not only his club members but other people as well would be sorely tempted to miss Mass for the pleasure of watching the acrobat. And he knew, too, there was no point in reasoning with the man.

"I'll challenge you on any of your acts," he told him. "With a wager, too. If I win, not only will I get the money we bet, but you will clear out of here." John beat the professional at jumping, juggling and climbing. Since the stakes were doubled at each new contest, the acrobat lost a considerable amount of money, and, fearing even more losses, begged off the remaining contests.

"I'll tell you what we shall do," John suggested, "join us for Mass, and we shall have you as our guest for dinner at my cousin's restaurant. We might even end up giving you back some of the money."

As he walked toward the church, the mollified acrobat wondered: "Who is this boy who conquers your heart with the same ease with which he wins a bet?"

"Which Way, Lord?"

Toward the end of his college course, as he surveyed the future, John felt confused. Something seemed to pull him away from the world around him. At times, kneeling in some of Chieri's beautiful churches, he would muse: "God wants me, this much I know. I know, too, that I want to do things for Him, for people—young people especially. But how, where, Lord?"

For a time, the life and spirit of St. Francis of Assisi seemed to hold what he thought was the answer to his searchings. 'I'll become a Franciscan," he decided, and told his friends about it. They were dismayed. John Bosco in a monastery?

"What in the world is John up to?" Don Dessano, Castelnuovo's new and popular pastor said to himself upon hearing the news. He sent for Margaret, hoping she could convince her son to change his mind.

"Margaret," the determined priest told her, "that boy does not have to go to a monastery in order to become a priest. What's wrong with being a priest like me? If he becomes a monk, you'll probably never see him again. And what's going to become of you? You are not getting any younger, and you'll end up being alone with no support whatever. If I know your John, I know you are the only one who can make him change his mind."

Margaret thanked Don Dessano, went back to Becchi, donned her Sunday dress and was off to Chieri.

"What brings you here, Mom?" a surprised John greeted her.

"Johnny, I hear you decided to go to a monastery. All I want to know is that you are sure of your decision. Have no thought about me. God and your soul come first. I don't expect anything from you, really. I was born poor, am living poor, and mean to die poor. If, God forbid, you should ever become rich, I am afraid you'll never see me again."

John was deeply moved. "I can't tell you, Mom," he said, "what your visit, your words, mean to me. All I ask is that you pray for me."

"You know I always do, Johnny." She embraced him fondly. "And now I return to Becchi feeling a whole lot better."

Knowing that his friend and confidant, Don Giuseppe Cafasso, was in nearby Turin, John went to him with his problem. The priest everyone in Turin called a "saint" listened to him, then said slowly, deliberately: "John, surely the Lord wants you, but not in a monastery. Go right on with your studies, in the Seminary."

"You Are Now a Priest!"

"Summa cum Laude!" The Rector of the Seminary

said in resounding Latin as he presented John Bosco with his diploma. Though now joyously anticipating his ordination, John left the Seminary with more than a tinge of sadness. The best years of his life were spent under its roof—years of growth, of peace, and of lasting friendships. "I felt I was everyone's friend," he wrote in his memoirs, revealing a facet of his own warm and outgoing personality.

There was a touch of simplicity and of intimacy to the ordination ceremony on June 5, 1841. It was held in the private chapel of the Archbishop's residence in Turin. John had preferred it so, and Archbishop Fransoni, who had taken a great personal interest in him, was only too happy to comply with John's desire.

All the festivities were kept for his first Mass in his native parish church at Castelnuovo. The banquet, held at the parish house in honor of the new priest, was attended by John's relatives, the neighboring clergy, and friends from the entire countryside. The eyes of all were on the new priest and on his proud mother, who was seated by him, but they could only surmise what lay behind their smiling faces often streaked with tears of happiness.

Later in the evening of that memorable day, when all the guests had left and mother and son were finally in their humble Becchi cottage, they must have talked of the past, of their combined troubles and sufferings, since John, in his scant memoirs, wrote that he could not help but say to Margaret, "Aren't God's ways wonderful, Mother?" But Margaret reminded him that the joyful day of his ordination was only the beginning of the longer, harder road that lay ahead.

"John, my son," she said, "you are now a priest! You

will offer Mass daily, but remember that in your life Mass and suffering will go together. It may not be so now, but you'll know some day that your mother was right. I ask only that you pray for me. From now on, think only of helping people and saving souls; don't worry about me."

CHAPTER V

GIVE ME THE YOUNG

"Where Do I Start?"

Shortly after his ordination, Don Bosco—such was now his official name—had another heart-to-heart talk with his friend and advisor Don Cafasso. "I have been offered all kinds of positions," he told him. "I have even been asked to remain at Castelnuovo as assistant pastor. But, Father, you know that it's young people I want to work for. Where do I start?"

"Come to Turin," the good priest suggested. "There are plenty of youngsters here who need care. You can stay with me here at St. Francis' Priests House. The rest will come. . ."

It came sooner than expected, just a short few weeks after he arrived in Turin where he found the lot of many young people even worse than he had anticipated. On Dec. 8, feast of the Immaculate Conception, he was vesting for Mass in the Church of St. Francis of Assisi when he suddenly heard the sexton's voice, loud and menacing: "What are you doing here if you can't serve Mass?" And then a boy's timid reply, "It's cold out. . ." The sexton again, "Does that mean you can come to the sacristy? Out, boy, out of here and be quick about it!" He threatened the boy with a broom, drove him out, and slammed the door.

Don Bosco had barely time to take in the scene. "Joseph," he called to the sexton, "what are you doing to that boy? He is my friend! Call him back. . ."

Grumbling, the sexton did as he was told and, with some difficulty, managed to persuade the boy to come back. Ill-clad and shivering, the youth stood before Don Bosco. "Stay for Mass," the priest told him gently, "and afterwards we can talk."

Bartholomew Garelli was the boy's name. He was sixteen, an orphan, and an apprentice bricklayer from Asti.

"Where do you live, Bartholomew?"

"With some friends in a garret not far from here. . ."

"I suppose you can read and write. . ." The boy shook his head sadly. "I don't know anything," he said.

"Can you sing?" the priest asked. The boy stared at him. "What a strange question!" he thought.

"Can you whistle?" The boy laughed. Immediately they were friends. Some more gentle probing, and the boy bared his life to Don Bosco. He had been left as a child in the care of neighbors after his parents had died, and had been a farm-boy until a few days previously. No instruction whatever; no school and no church, either.

"Bartholomew, would you be willing to come if I were to teach you privately?"

"Of course I would. Gladly."

"Bart, one more thing: When you come, bring some of your friends with you."

He came back in a few days with six of his friends. In a few weeks they were close to one hundred. Like Garelli, they were mostly from the countryside. They had come to the city in search of jobs, but had found trouble, too. Don Cafasso was delighted to welcome them, and so were most of the priests of St. Francis' House, who thought nothing of giving up their Sunday quiet. Don Bosco's new activities at the residence were certainly not without an element of noise. The youngsters spent all day there on Sundays. They were instructed, fed, and encouraged to play to their heart's content. Often Don Bosco took them out for excursions to the surrounding hills. The sight of a young priest walking the Turin streets with a mob of noisy boys was a rather new experience for Turin's staid citizens.

Soon Don Bosco gave his young friends most of his time, keeping them company on their free days, finding them work with decent employers, visiting them in their homes or lodgings; and often, too, providing them with food and clothes. Their number grew steadily. St. Francis' House was no longer adequate. Don Cafasso once again came to the rescue.

"How Much More Can I Take?"

"Marchesa Barolo has the place for you, Don Bosco. Her institution has spacious grounds and fine buildings. She is quite willing to have the boys there, but on condition that you become chaplain of her establishment." There was a pleading tone to Don Cafasso's words.

"What can I say, Father?" Don Bosco replied. "I am not really happy about being chaplain; but, if it helps our boys, I accept, of course."

Marchesa Giulia de Colbert Barolo was the *grande dame* of the Piedmontese aristocracy. Widowed and without children, she had invested her wealth in a large institution comprised of a hospital, a rehabilitation center for girls, and a convent for the Sisters of Charity who ran the establishment. She had met Don Bosco, and wondered why such a brilliant young priest should give so much of his time to those ragged, noisy street boys. Charitable and devout, she was quite willing to open the doors of her place to that motley crowd of ragamuffins if it but made her new chaplain happy. Little did she know what three hundred young adolescents could do to the quiet, solemn atmosphere of her institution.

"How much more can I take?" she complained to Don Bosco after eight months of what she termed "an impossible situation." "It's your choice, Father," she continued bluntly, "either your 'Oratory,' as you call it, or my place. . ."

"Madame," Don Bosco replied, "you have been most truly kind and gracious, and I can never thank you enough for what you did for my boys; but you might know that my choice lies with the boys. All I ask is that you give me time to find a new place."

"The magnanimous *Marchesa* gave Don Bosco not only the time he needed but also her continued support for as long as she lived.

"I See Thousands of Boys."

For several months Don Bosco and his boys were chased from pillar to post. Undaunted, he tried meeting with them in a public park where they could play and then assemble for Mass in a church any one of his priest friends might put at his disposal. The police intervened when complaints poured in from disgruntled citizens, who said he was creating a nuisance with his boys.

"See if you can rent a field somewhere and be on your own," Don Cafasso suggested. He even supplied the money for the rent. They were indeed on their own for several weeks in a large field in the Turin Valdocco region. The place was isolated, and no one seemed to care what Don Bosco's boys did until the owners of the field, the Filippi brothers, one day noticed that the grass in their field was being trampled by those sturdy feet to the point of no return.

"Sorry, Don Bosco. We shall end up with no hay for our horses. The premises must be vacated on or before Palm Sunday. We are ready to forget all about the rent, but we can't afford to let that field go to ruin."

"Where to now, Lord?" was Don Bosco's silent and anguished question.

But other questions were being asked concerning Don Bosco himself by some of his friends—and by Father Borel, of all people. They wondered whether Don Bosco was not beginning to show signs of mental instability. It all started when Father Borel, who had been one of his most valued assistants, one day told him that, in the face of so many difficulties, it might be wiser for him to reconsider his plans. "Why don't you cut down the number of boys?" Don Borel suggested. "Limit yourself to twenty or so—the most promising, or those most in need—and go back to St. Francis' House."

"Don Borel,"—there was dismay in Don Bosco's voice—"you speak of twenty boys when I see thousands of them. . I see a great big school, not far from here, with beautiful buildings, large courtyards, a magnificent church. . .I see classrooms; I see training shops for those boys; I see priests and brothers, sisters and laymen by the hundreds instructing them—and not just here, but all over the world. . ."

Don Borel was shocked. "My poor Don Bosco! What's happening to you? It has just been too much for you. You do need a rest. . ."

"So Young, So Popular!"

Word spread quickly that Don Bosco was going mad. Poor Don Bosco! So young, so popular, so full of zeal! How sad that he should ruin himself over those ignorant, ragged, noisy young vandals! But, then, he was always a little strange, wasn't he?

Some of his priest friends decided that a few weeks' rest was what he needed. Two canons from the cathedral volunteered to handle the delicate situation. After making arrangements for a room in the local asylum, they went to visit him one day at his residence.

"Join us for a ride, Don Bosco," one of them suggested. "It is a beautiful day, and we have a carriage waiting."

"I will, gladly!" Don Bosco replied. "But first," he continued with a sly smile, "there is something I should like to discuss with you, confidentially, of course!" And he plunged into his grandiose plans and dreams, describing in detail what he expected to achieve.

"You mean you intend to found a religious order to take care of those boys?" one of the canons inquired.

"Indeed I do. I have even thought of the habit the members will wear: overalls, gentlemen, overalls and shirt-sleeves, since they will have a lot of work to do." They knew Don Bosco was speaking in dead earnest.

"Shouldn't we talk about all this while riding around the city?"

"Of course," Don Bosco replied. He picked up his hat and accompanied them to the carriage.

"Get in, Father."

"Oh now, not before my seniors. You first, Fathers." No sooner were they seated than he slammed the door shut and called to the coachman. "Quick," he shouted, "to the asylum! These two gentlemen are expected there!"

There were hearty laughs all over Turin, and it was not Don Bosco's madness people talked about for days afterwards.

"Who Rang the Bells?"

Palm Sunday dawned and found Don Bosco and his few assistants in the Filippi field, waiting for the boys. They knew this would be the last time in that place.

"We shall have the boys for Mass at the Church of Our Lady of the Fields," Don Bosco told his helpers. "The Capuchin Fathers are preparing lunch for them. We shall then come back here for our afternoon program."

"What about next Sunday?" Father Borel inquired. Don Bosco opened his arms and sighed. "God only knows," he said.

The boys, nearly four hundred strong, marched through the quiet city streets, chattering away in subdued tones, to the steady beat of the drums in the lead. Turning off the main boulevard, they started up the hill toward the monastery church. All of a sudden the bells in the church tower began to ring joyously, wildly, surprising all the countryside. The boys had visited there a number of times, but never had they been made welcome by the ringing of bells. Never before had anyone heard those bells peal so jubilantly.

"Who's ringing the bells?" the monks were all asking one another. By the time some of them got to the tower, the bells had stopped, and no one was there. "Who rang the bells?" was the question on everyone's lips all through the day. "One of Don Bosco's tricks," someone suggested. "No, the angels," others said. . .

Back in the Filippi field the boys soon lost their zest for play. They milled around Don Bosco. "Where to, next week, Father?" they would ask; or "What's going to happen to our Oratory?"

"We'll find a place," Don Bosco assured them while in his heart he prayed, "Lord, tell me what to do, where to look!"

"Can It Be?"

He did not have to look very far. With all those youngsters around him, Don Bosco had not noticed the man at his side, who for sometime had been trying to get his attention. Raising his voice, "May I speak to you, Father?" the man finally asked. "I hear you are looking for property in which to establish a laboratory. . ."

"Not a laboratory," Don Bosco answered distractedly, "an Oratory."

"Oratory or laboratory, it doesn't matter. But if you are interested, you better hurry and see the owner. Pinardi is the name, there across the road. I'll take you to him."

It was only a shed, a sort of hayloft with a dirt floor and with a roof that seemed about to collapse at any minute. Not much land around it, but suitable for a start. The price was reasonable. Pinardi swore he would make repairs, "and," he added, "if some of those husky boys give me a hand, I'll have things ready for you by next Sunday."

"Can it be? Yes, it is! Lord, you did it; you did it for me and for my boys!" Don Bosco's thoughts were in a happy turmoil as he rushed back to the Filippi field. He clapped his hands and assembled the boys. "Listen to me," he shouted, his voice breaking with emotion, "listen to me: Next Sunday, Easter Sunday, I expect to see you all over there at the Pinardi shed, right across from here. Now we have a place of our own! Nothing much yet, but give us a little time and watch it grow. See you there next Sunday for a wonderful day!"

There were deafening shouts of "Viva Don Bosco!" Then suddenly a few of the older boys picked him up as if he were a feather, and carried him around the field in triumph.

CHAPTER VI

ON THE MARCH

"I Have No One, Father."

To the transformed Pinardi shed, inaugurated on Easter Sunday amidst the Alleluias of his boys, Don Bosco soon added a fairly solid structure on a much larger piece of property. By the end of 1846, the Oratory had become a beehive of activity. The program was now expanded to include regular evening classes and recreational pursuits while Sundays saw more than seven hundred youngsters spend most of the day with Don Bosco. But the Oratory was not yet what he had dreamed it to be, a place boys could call home.

He became increasingly concerned with young men who were totally abandoned to themselves, without a home, often unable to get jobs for lack of any skill. He had occasionally seen them in the streets in swearing, fighting groups. He had visited some of the hovels in which they lived and shared their wretched sleeping quarters with depraved men and criminals. And he had seen some of them in the city prisons. For these boys he dreamed of clean, airy buildings with spacious courtyards, dormitories, classrooms, workshops particularly, where a boy could learn to be a printer, a bookbinder, a cobbler, a machinist, a carpenter, a stone mason without leaving the grounds. He dreamed, hoped, prayed, and waited.

43

Late one cold, rainy night, a sixteen-year old boy, in tatters and soaked to the skin, knocked at his door.

"Come in, lad. It's no night to be out in weather like this. Where are you coming from?"

"From Valsesia, Father."

"That's a good many miles away. What are you doing in Turin?"

"I am a mason-apprentice, looking for a job. I've spend the three liras I had, and. . ." He was on the verge of tears.

"You mean you don't know where to go?"

"I have no one, Father."

"You have me, now," Don Bosco assured him with a smile. "Your name?"

"Michael, Michael Fassio."

"Come, Michael. First a change of clothing, next a nice bowl of minestrone, and then we'll go scouting for a bed."

There were no beds. Don Bosco took his own mattress and placed it on the kitchen floor. "It will do for tonight," he said. "Say a prayer, Michael, and have a good rest."

His own bed was far from comfortable without the mattress, but he did not mind it at all. For the first time he was sharing his home with a boy!

Six months later, nearly thirty youngsters were calling the Oratory their home.

"And Leave Becchi, John?"

In the fall of 1846, Don Bosco spent several days at Becchi, recuperating from a serious bout with pneumonia. He was pleased to note how remarkably well his mother

looked; how vigorous and active she was in spite of her
advancing age. Quite suddenly one day he surprised her with
a question. "Mother, would you be willing to come to
Turin with me?"

"And what would I be doing in Turin, John?"

"I need you to help me with my boys."

"But you do have helpers there, John: teachers,
assistants. . ."

"Yes, but those boys need a mother."

Margaret looked at her son for a few moments in silence.
She thought of her cottage, her fields, Joseph and his family,
the friends she had known all her life, the scenes of her
childhood. . . .She was about to say, "And leave Becchi,
John?" when she realized there could be only one sensible
answer. "John," she said calmly, "if you feel this is what the
Lord wants, I am ready. I can leave when you leave."

She got busy packing: a few pots and pans, a supply
of flour and fruits. Her personal things she packed separately,
including her wedding dress and the little trinkets she had
gathered through the years. Joseph would cart everything
to Turin later, since Don Bosco was anxious to leave for the
Oratory as soon as possible.

The day was unusually bright and warm, so they decided
to walk to Chieri and then proceed from there to Turin by
coach. But after a brief stop at cousin Pianta's restaurant in
Chieri, they felt Turin was not that far, and a leisurely walk
not too inconvenient. It was getting dark by the time they
reached Turin's Valdocco section where the Oratory was
located. They ran into Don Vola, a priest friend of Don
Bosco, who occasionally helped with the Oratory youngsters.

"Don Bosco, how are you? I am delighted to see you

back in Turin. And with your mother, too!" He touched the brim of his hat and bowed to Margaret. "Where are you coming from?"

"From Becchi, Don Vola. A bit tired and dusty from the long walk, as you see."

"You mean you walked all the way from Becchi?"

"The day was fine, and the coach too expensive. . . ."

"I should have known that, Don Bosco. Money is always your problem." The good priest reached into his vest pocket, and out came a gold watch and chain. "I haven't any cash with me," he said. "Here, take this. I have another watch home."

Mother and son resumed their walk toward the Oratory. "See, Mother, how the Lord provides! Here is something that will bring us a bit of money. It is a sign, too, that Providence is not about to let us down."

"Has it ever, John?" Margaret whispered.

"I'll Never Walk Out on Him."

One look at the place, and Margaret knew the Oratory needed a mother. The kitchen and the bedrooms were her first concern until she noticed how poorly furnished the chapel was. She quietly took her wedding dress apart and cut it into vestments. Her best linens she turned into altar cloths. Everything she had was converted into something useful for the service of the Lord or for John's boys.

Still, there were hardships aplenty. She wanted to lighten her son's burdens, but wondered at times if she was not adding to them. How could she dare complain to him when she saw him come home so weary every night after tramping the streets, begging, visiting his boys on their jobs, doing favors to all sorts of people. But she had no choice. Always, there was something amiss.

"John," she would say to him, "all I have is potatoes. How can I make minestrone without pasta, beans, meat, oil?. . .John, the baker says he hasn't been paid for last month's bread. He refuses to deliver even one single loaf. . . . John, please, no more boys. We don't have a bed, or a place for a bed, either. . . ."

And those youngsters, who looked, and prayed, and sang like angels—were they not sometimes positive little devils?

"John, I hate to tell you, but this has to stop. One day they pull down my wash because they need a rope, and trample all my clean wash in the mud. Next is their clothing: Look at them, no wonder they are always in rags! And who does the mending?. . .When they take off their shoes and socks, they throw them in a pile; I have to pick them up and match the pairs. . ."

Playing their favorite war game, one day, they tore into her beautiful vegetable garden, trampling her tomato plants, cabbage and lettuce, and prized zucchini.

"John, I am going back to Becchi," she told him late that night when he came to see her in the kitchen, as was his custom, before retiring. "I have done all I could. I have tried. I just don't think I can go on."

He was too moved to speak. "Mother," he whispered, "look," and pointed to the crucifix on the kitchen wall.

"I am sorry, John. I was so upset!" She wiped her eyes with the corner of her apron. "You know well enough that I'll never walk out on Him or on you!"

"You Are All Angels. . ."

There were happy days, too, in the life of the Oratory's one and only Mama Margaret. Every year, on her nameday, she was made to sit on a high chair, like a queen on her throne. All her "little devils" surrounded her; they sang and made eloquent speeches; gave her flowers and promised prayers, until she could hardly restrain her tears.

"You are all angels," she would say at the end of the entertainment, "and you know I love you almost as much as Don Bosco does." And, turning to him, "Father, tonight, shouldn't they all get a special dessert—chocolate mousse and pastry—as on Christmas Day?"

Occasionally some unexpected event brightened her busy schedule. She was shredding cabbage in the kitchen, one day, when Don Bosco dropped in to see her with Count Sclopis, his friend and benefactor.

Introducing her, "My mother," Don Bosco said to the Count. "There is not a cook like her in the whole city of Turin."

"I might be even better," Margaret laughed, "if I had some meat to go with the cabbage."

"Signora, tell me, what are some of the dishes you prepare for your youngsters?" the Count inquired.

"I throw everything in that big pot, Signor Conte. Minestrone, almost every day, if you really must know. . ."

"But don't you have someone to help you?"

"Some of those little rascals, but only when I really

need them."

"What I mean, Signora, is that you should have an assistant cook."

"I most certainly have one. And quite a help.he is, too! Today he happens to be busy with other things. . ."

"And who, may I ask, is your assistant cook?"

"There he is!" Mama Margaret said, pointing to Don Bosco with her kitchen knife. "Signor Conte," she continued, "you should see him work on the specialty of the house, *Polenta a la Piemontese*!" And she chuckled away as she turned to her cabbage.

It was only after she was done with the dishes that she discovered the envelope that the Count had deftly left on the kitchen table. She ran to Don Bosco. "Look, John, what the Count left for me on the kitchen table. One thousand liras!"

"That should pay most of our bills," Don Bosco replied.

"But, John, what about the new stove, the pots and pans you promised me for so long?. . ."

"All right, Mother. We'll go half-and-half."

The Mysterious Banker

"Don Bosco's dreams have a curious knack of coming true." These words were all the more significant because they were pronounced at a clergy meeting, in 1856, by a leading Turin prelate who, for several years, had been very critical of Don Bosco. He reported to the assembled clergymen that he had visited the Oratory in the fall.

"I could hardly believe my eyes," he told them. I saw

beautiful buildings, including a lovely church, playgrounds, classrooms, training shops for all sorts of trades. Even more astounding, I found the place teeming with boys as cheerful and well-behaved as one would wish all our Turin youth to be."

"Who assists Don Bosco in all this work?" one of the priests asked.

"I saw dozens of men, incredibly young; most of them, I was told, trained by Don Bosco himself from among his own youngsters. Some of them are dressed like seminarians and are evidently full-time teachers and assistants. It would seem that Don Bosco is also quite successful in recruiting part-time instructors who give freely of their time, particularly in the night-school program. He has his mother, too, at the Oratory; an extraordinary woman who, for years, has been involved with his work. The boys love her dearly."

"Does Don Bosco aim to establish some sort of religious order to carry on his work?" another clergyman queried.

"This is quite evident," replied the prelate, "since he has actually named his assistants 'Salesians.' " The Oratory itself, as you know, is named after Saint Francis de Sales. I am told he intends to open Oratories outside Turin, too."

Finally, the inevitable question: "Where does Don Bosco find the money to support his establishment?"

"The prelate paused briefly. "Frankly," he said, "it is the one thing I can't tell you. He has friends, of course. Even Marchesa Barolo is known to help him. I have heard from a reliable source that King Victor Emmanuel himself is among his benefactors. Don Bosco is a very enterprising man. You know about his lotteries, I am sure. But it takes hundreds of thousands of liras to carry such an establishment as the

Oratory. One of his assistants, a wiry young seminarian, Michael Rua by name, told me that Don Bosco has a mysterious banker to whom he goes whenever he needs money. I pressed him to tell me his name. You would not believe it; but, with utter simplicity, the young man answered: "The Madonna, of course!"

The prelate concluded with a quizzical smile: "As you see, gentlemen, we are not just faced with strange dreams that come true, but with miracles, too."

Mama Margaret Goes Home

Toward the end of November, 1856, Mama Margaret lay dying of pneumonia. The Oratory boys were disconsolate. They stormed heaven with their prayers. They lingered under the window of her room, unwilling to play or even leave; many of them in tears. Whenever Don Bosco appeared in their midst, they surrounded him quietly; the one question, more in their eyes than on their lips: "How is Mama?" And Don Bosco would calmly reply, "All we can do is pray, boys, and I know you do."

Don Bosco spent long hours by her bed, trying to restrain his tears. Shortly after midnight, on November 25, Margaret fixed her eyes first on Joseph, and then on John. "John," she whispered: "Leave me now. It hurts me to see you so broken up. Go get some rest. Your brother is here with me. Go now, John." He kissed and blessed her, still unwilling to leave. "Please, John, go."

Shortly before dawn, Joseph entered Don Bosco's room. "John," he sobbed, "Mama is. . ." and buried his face on the priest's shoulder. At 5:30, Don Bosco left the Oratory with one of his boys to go to the Consolata Church, Margaret's favorite shrine of the Madonna. He offered Mass for the repose of her soul, and, before he left the church, knelt at Our Lady's altar. "My youngsters and I have lost our mother," he prayed. "Dear Madonna, do take her place and be our mother from now on!"

CHAPTER VII

THE SALESIAN WAY

"A Drop of Honey. . ."

"Louis, did you ever stop to think that the Lord loves you and wants you to be happy, and I mean really happy, and I mean really happy here and hereafter?" To the confused adolescent these words of Don Bosco came like a breath of fresh air. In later years, recounting his first meeting and conversation with Don Bosco, the youth, who became Father Louis Fassio, said: "It may seem strange, but I had never thought of religion as something intended to make me happy. The priests I had known had always been solemn, distant, even forbidding. What they preached was certainly not anything to make a boy happy."

For young Louis and his three hundred or so compaions, religion came easy at the Oratory. It was part of a life in which everything seemed to be geared to make one happy. It was, and everyone knew it, Don Bosco's way.

"Father, what do you hope to accomplish with those young vandals of yours?" Marchesa Barolo pointedly asked him when he had refused to give up his boys and accept to remain as chaplain of her institution.

"I would expect, Signora Marchesa," he replied, "that most of them will turn out to be honest citizens, and eventually earn for themselves a corner in heaven." One could hardly ask for more. Don Bosco did: in the way in which this was to be done. He called it the Salesian way.

"I shall try to carry with me everywhere the charity and gentleness of St. Francis de Sales. May his charity enlighten my every step." With these words, which he wrote a few days before his ordination, Don Bosco meant to make the gentle Bishop of Geneva his model and guide. He admired in him the zealous missionary, the tireless catechism teacher, the writer of books and pamphlets, his love for the poor. But it was his kindness and graciousness he especially prized. He would often quote his sayings: "Everything by love, nothing by force. . .More flies are caught with a drop of honey than with a barrel of vinegar. . .To speak well, we need only to love well. . .Good works done with love and joy are twice blessed."

It was not by accident that the Oratory was named after St. Francis de Sales as was the first church Don Bosco built. His spiritual children were to be known as "Salesians." He said: "De Sales' heart was most like the meek and gentle Heart of Jesus. I could wish for nothing better for myself and my followers."

"It Is Hardly a Secret."

The priest who came to see Don Bosco was a Spanish Jesuit, who might have modeled for an El Greco portrait. Tall and gaunt, one would think a smile had never crossed his face. He had been rector of several boarding schools for boys, but had never quite reconciled himself to what he termed "the atmosphere prevalent in our schools." He described it to Don Bosco as "an atmosphere of apathy and passive resistance on the part of the pupils, certainly not conducive to good character training."

"Father," he said, "what I note in your boys is just the reverse. They are open, self-confident, joyously free in their ways. . ."

"And probably much too noisy and overfriendly," Don Bosco interjected.

"It is what I would want my boys to be. Tell me, Don Bosco, what is your secret?"

"It is hardly a secret, my good Father," Don Bosco replied. "It is actually something as old as the Gospel."

The priest was all ears, expecting a lengthy dissertation on the most effective approach to Christian education.

"What you call a secret might best be described with one word: love!" Don Bosco continued.

A look of mild surprise spread over the earnest face of the priest. "Quite simply," Don Bosco said, "we must love those youngsters. I have no doubt that you do. But there is something which is just as important: the boys must know that we love them. Come, take a look out of that window. Note how the instructors mingle with those boys. They actually join them in their games. They do not consider themselves superiors. They are like fathers, brothers, friends to their charges. What you have here, Father, is not so much a school as a family."

Later in the evening, the good Jesuit Father was treated to a practical demonstration of Don Bosco's words. The members of the staff had barely left the supper table to rejoin the boys at their games, when the dining room was literally invaded by some thirty boys of the upper grades. They surrounded Don Bosco on every side, and for a few minutes the place was total bedlam. They vied to get Don Bosco's attention shouting, laughing, pushing to get close to him. It was some time before they finally quieted down to hear Don Bosco introduce the Jesuit to them. He then initiated a delightful dialogue with them, touching on the most trivial events of the day, to the amazement of the Reverend guest. He finally dismissed them, after treating them to what had been left of the dessert on the table.

"A scene like this," the Jesuit remarked, "is unthinkable in my school. I see, Don Bosco, that your Oratory is indeed first a family and then a school. I know your secret now."

"Aren't You My Friend?"

While most of the pupils at the Oratory were either orphan or destitute boys, there were some whose families or guardians could afford and willingly paid a nominal tuition fee, so that their youngsters might benefit from Don Bosco's educational method. Albert Caviglia was one of these. "Albert the Great," Don Bosco had nicknamed the bright Turinese lad who, small and sprightly, always managed to elbow his way to greet Don Bosco even when Father was hemmed in on every side by other boys.

One day Don Bosco found him in a corner, glum and disconsolate. "Why, Albert the Great, where is your smile today?"

On the verge of tears, the boy stammered about having to leave the Oratory since his parents could no longer afford the tuition.

"And who says you must leave the Oratory?" Don

Bosco inquired.

"Father Bursar. . ."

"Aren't you my friend, Albert?"

"Of course, I am, Father."

"Now listen to me, Albert: You are my friend, and Father Bursar is my friend. Don't you think the three of us can get together and settle this thing?"

"I guess so, Father. . ."

"Now, then, run along, and stop worrying, Albert. You will stay here whether or not your parents pay the tuition."

"Thank you, Father!" And a happy boy was off to play.

Albert, who became Father Albert Caviglia, one of the Salesian Society's outstanding historians, often remarked that Don Bosco's educational system aimed at the heart because it came from the heart.

Not All Angels

Signor Carlo Conestabile, a well-known Turin educator, had made the rounds of the Oratory and was back in Don Bosco's office. "I am quite impressed," he said. "What I find here is order without constraint. These youngsters, I noticed, are extremely well-behaved, and yet they are cheerful, friendly, exuberant. No small achievement for a boarding school of this size. But surely, Don Bosco, not all of them are angels. You must have your share of problem boys."

"We do, of course, Signor Conestabile. I have the names of some of them right here on my desk. Here is one, for instance, who is quite a troublemaker. I intend to speak to him today; not here in the office, but outside at recess time.

In fact, I might even invite him to take a walk with me in town. By the time we get through talking about trivial things, he will be quite ready and willing to open his heart to me. There may be something that troubles that youngster. I noticed that he has not been to the Sacraments for sometime. If we can get him back on his feet spiritually, the battle is more than half won."

"You do feel, Father, that religion is an important element in the character training of a boy. . ."

"I am convinced that it is the most important, the essential element in fact, Signor Conestabile." Don Bosco went on to explain that he did not think it was possible to educate a boy and prepare him for life without grounding him solidly on religion. "Where is a young man to find the motive and encouragement to walk the narrow path, if not in religion?" he asked. He was careful to point out that religion, as practiced at the Oratory, was joyous, vibrant and uplifting. "Not long ago," he added, "two English lords visited here and, like yourself, Signor Conestabile, were amazed that we are able to take care of so many youngsters with ease in an environment that banishes all sorts of punishment, and where expression and not repression is the rule. When told about the role religion plays among us, one of them said: "That certainly explains it. I think some people in London should hear about this."

It was at this point that Signor Conestabile added his own comment: "Not only in London, Don Bosco, but in many of our schools right here in Turin."

"Prevent. Do Not Repress."

"What good is it to repress disorders after they have taken place? Young people get into trouble more through lack of judgment than through malice." These were Don Bosco's constant refrains. The solution? "The educator must live exclusively for his young charges. He must share their interests and their games; he must assist them without imposing his assistance on them at any time. His presence in their midst must truly be like that of a father, a brother or a friend, who is there to prevent, never to repress."

"This is demanding a great deal of the educator," someone suggested. Don Bosco agreed and went on to explain that the Salesian educator was expected to be a person totally dedicated to his calling. This meant that he should freely consecrate his life to God, whom he chooses to serve in the person of the young, particularly the neglected. To most people who lived close to Don Bosco, the success of his method of education needed little explaining. He exemplified it in his every move.

"He was truly a 'father' to us," wrote Father Philip Rinaldi, one of his youngsters who later became his close collaborator and successor as head of the Salesian Society. "We always felt at ease with him; we never found him too busy to listen to us, who were often crude, tattered and not very clean. . .He made each of us feel as if he were his favorite. With us, he shared his joys and sorrows, his plans and ideas. To him, we went freely; to him, we spoke freely. He opened his heart to us as easily as he opened the door of his room. Even if we complained to him about something, as children are likely to do with their father, we always found him eager to listen, kind and understanding."

Father Rinaldi never forgot what Don Bosco told him when, as a young headmaster, he once went to him with one of his problems. "Remember, Philip," he told him, "what cannot be obtained through love is not worth getting in any other way. In dealing with young people, love is the only key that opens the door."

CHAPTER VIII

"GOD" IS ITS NAME

" 'A Saint' Did You Say?"

In the early days of the Oratory when Marchesa Barolo was told that Don Bosco had moved to Valdocco and was living in what might be best described as a shack, her first reaction was one of dismay.

"I gave up trying to understand that man," she told her friend Countess Riccardi. "Here is a priest who was doing wonders as our chaplain. We loved him dearly. Why he chose to leave us and embroil himself with those young vandals I shall never understand. Of course, I intend to help his Oratory. I feel truly sorry for him. But can you explain to me why in the world such a promising young priest should be throwing his life away for those ragamuffins?"

Countess Riccardi was nonplussed, but essayed a reply. "Wouldn't you think, my dear Marchesa, that he must be some kind of saint to be taking on such work?"

" 'A saint,' did you say? Perhaps, but a strange and unusual saint. I am told that he was recently seen drinking with a group of young rowdies in one of those wretched Valdocco taverns. And I don't think his fund-raising methods are very commendable, either. No, I tell you, I shall never be able to understand Don Bosco!"

Countess Riccardi did not quite know what to say this time, so again she put her words in the form of a question.

"My dear Marquise, does anyone ever understand saints?"

"Leave Him Alone!"

There were others whose feelings about "that Valdocco priest" were far more hostile than those expressed by Marchesa Barolo. Many of Don Bosco's own fellow priests were openly critical of him. They once told Don Cafasso that his protege was a disgrace to the Turin clergy.

For the first time, they saw the calm, soft-spoken Don Cafasso in a burst of anger. "Leave Don Bosco alone!" he told them bluntly. "I see you do not recognize a saint when you see one. There is not a priest in Turin who does the Lord's work as Don Bosco does. Leave him alone, I say!"

Most of the people in Turin who knew Don Bosco were not ready to call him a saint. They thought of him simply as a good priest with a consuming interest in neglected youngsters. They could not help but like this young priest of medium height, well-built, with thick, dark-chestnut hair, whose pleasant face was always brightened by a smile and whose words were friendly, warm and full of humor. "There is no other priest in Turin quite like him," they used to say as they saw him running here, there, and everywhere, and forever surrounded by youngsters.

But a dimension was slowly emerging in Don Bosco's personality which could not escape his close associates as they watched him struggle to realize his life-long dream. This man, they discovered, was being led by the Lord to whom he, in turn, was making himself available with all the energy of his soul. He was, they knew, truly a man of God.

Six Copper Coins

"So much energy and so much calm!" a visiting bishop once remarked after what he had described as an "unforgettable" interview with Don Bosco.

"I think I can explain it," the prelate added. "Don Bosco has a keen sense of his mission. His whole energy is deployed to effect what he knows is God's purpose for him. He is convinced that once he does all in his power to bring it to pass, the Lord will do the rest."

Don Bosco's life is filled with events that bear out the bishop's keen appraisal. One such event is particularly relevant. In 1863, he set his hand to the building of a great church at the Oratory in honor of the Lady of his dreams: Our Lady Help of Christians—Don Bosco's favorite title for the Lord's Mother. It was to become a center of devotion and the mother church of the Salesian Society. The story of its building is one of a cash box always empty and yet always replenished by some miraculous means. When construction was about to start, the contractor came to him for an advance to cover the expenses for the month.

"Here," said Don Bosco, "it's all I have at the moment. Open your hands." And he emptied his purse in the astonished builder's hands. Six cents!

"Don't worry," added Don Bosco with a smile. "Our Lady will surely find the money for her church. I am only her cashier."

The truth is that, for nearly six years, he gave himself no rest, raising funds for the shrine of his beloved Madonna. When the magnificent structure was dedicated in 1868, it was completely paid for. "Every brick, every stone was a miracle of Our Lady," he himself said at the inaugural ceremony. He was sure the building of the church had been part of his mission. The Lord and his holy mother saw it through because he did his part.

It was the pattern of his entire life. The multitude of activities and the incredible achievements that crowned his efforts are likely to hide from us the man who was responsible for them. But the keen observer will not stop at what is purely exterior. He knows that the mainspring of Don Bosco's dynamic and successful activity can be found only in his soul and that its name is "God." Father Philip Rinaldi's assessment of what he calls the secret of Don Bosco's life is worth quoting.

"We shall never understand Don Bosco were we to ignore that he was a man who literally lived in God and for God. It is not in his astounding achievements that we must see the true face of the beloved Founder. Were it so, we might think of him purely as a man of purposeless action. Though untiring in his activity, his strength to create and achieve had but one source: his abiding union with God."

Nothing Finer

The word "miracle" was not a word Don Bosco used very often. He certainly never used it to describe the extraordinary things that took place through and around him. True to his peasant stock, he had an innate feeling for humility.

"What is the finest thing you ever saw?" he once asked a group of boys during recreation.

"Don Bosco," was the immediate reply of one of them.

"You remind me," replied Don Bosco, "of a good farmer who came to look at the prizes of our last lottery. While everyone was admiring some work of art, he stood with his eyes fixed on a huge sausage. He could see nothing finer than that!"

He never made any secret of his humble origin. In Paris, after a triumphant welcome by the city, he was given a reception at one of the city's most aristocratic homes. "Do you remember," he asked a friend within hearing of his hosts, "the narrow path running up from the road to Buttigliera and leading to a little hill? On that hill is a modest cottage with a tiny field below. That is my mother's house, and the field is where I used to tend the family cow. All these fine people, who are overwhelming me with their compliments, never think for a moment that they are honoring a former cowherd."

It is indeed remarkable that the marvelous should be found in the life of this humble and uncomplicated man, but even more remarkable that he should make it look as if he himself had very little to do with it.

A Mysterious Dog

All sorts of attempts have been made to account for the presence of a mysterious dog in his life. Those who saw it described it as a huge Dalmatian, standing about three feet high and of ferocious mien. Don Bosco himself recounts in his memoirs how Grigio (the grey one) first made its appearance.

"I was late coming home one evening and quite afraid, as I was walking on a dark street in one of the least reputable sections of Valdocco. Suddenly a large dog bounded silently to my side, and I must say that I was frightened for a moment. But he was not at all threatening; acting, in fact, like a dog that has just recognized its master. We soon made friends and he followed me as far as the Oratory. From then on, Grigio, as I had named him, kept me company every now and then, sometimes providentially. . .

"Toward the end of November, 1854, one stormy night I was returning from town. I thought it wise to take the road from the Consolata to the Cottolengo Institute, knowing that I would likely meet others on the road. At one point, I noticed that two men were walking some distance in front of me, keeping pace with me. I crossed to the other side to avoid them, but they did likewise. I then tried to walk back; but it was too late, for they suddenly turned around and in two steps they jumped me. Without a word, they threw some kind of coat over me. I struggled in vain to set myself free. One of them then tried to gag me with a scarf. I wanted to shout, but was unable to make a sound.

"It was then that Grigio appeared growling like a bear, and hurled himself at one of the men, while snarling at the other. 'Call off your dog!' they shouted, almost paralyzed with fear. 'I will, if you but learn your lesson and leave people alone!' Grigio kept on barking furiously even after I called him. The ruffians made off as fast as they could, and Grigio accompanied me to the Cottolengo where I stopped to recover a little. . .Then I made my way to the Oratory, this time under safe escort.

"Every evening when I ventured out into this deserted

quarter alone, I always noticed Grigio on one or the other side of the road. He was quite friendly with the Oratory boys, who often played with him. On one occasion, the dog arrived at the Oratory while we were at supper. He came right into the dining room where he was offered food, but the dog would not touch it. I remember that that evening I had returned rather late and that a friend had given me a lift in his carriage; it seemed that Grigio wanted to make sure that nothing had happened to me."

It was a strange animal. One evening it flatly refused to allow Don Bosco to leave the house, lying across the threshold and growling whenever he tried to pass. "If you won't listen to me, listen to the dog," remarked his mother. "It has more sense than you. ' A quarter of an hour later, a neighbor came in to say that he had heard of a plot to waylay Don Bosco that night. When attempts to harm Don Bosco ceased, the dog disappeared and was not seen again, save once, in 1883, when, late one stormy night, Don Bosco, accompanied by one of his priests, arrived at the station of Bordighera, and, finding no one to direct him to the Salesian House, was wandering in the dark, trying to find his way. He was suddenly startled by a bark, and Grigio appeared and led both priests to the house. "All sorts of stories have been told about this dog," wrote Don Bosco in his memoirs, "but I never discovered who his master was; all I know is that amid the many dangers that threatened me, this animal gave me providential protection."

When one day, at a friend's house in Marseilles, Don Bosco was recounting the dog's sudden appearance at Bordighera, in 1883, it was pointed out to him that his Grigio by then must have been three or four times the normal age of a dog. Don Bosco smiled and said, "if it wasn't Grigio, it was his son or even his grandson."

"God Will Send the Rest"

Life at the Oratory proved too rugged for young Francis Dalmazzo who, prior to his father's death, had been used to all the comforts of a fine home. On the day his mother was due to come to take him home, Francis decided to make his confession to Don Bosco for the last time. There were many for confession that morning, and his turn did not come until the rest of the community was about to go to breakfast. He was just beginning his confession when one of his companions came and whispered to Don Bosco that there was no bread for breakfast. Don Bosco calmly told him to see the bursar, whose responsibility it was. The boy was soon back to inform Don Bosco that the baker had positively refused to deliver any more bread unless payment was made for previous deliveries.

"I see," came the answer. "Get whatever bread is available and put it into the large basket, and God will send the rest. I'll come and give it out myself."

Dalmazzo was struck particularly by the words "God will send the rest," and followed Don Bosco to the side door of the church to see what he would do. He had heard some talk about the wonderful things done by him. "I found a place," he related, "where I could take in the scene, just behind Don Bosco, who was preparing to distribute the rolls to the four hundred boys as they lined up on their way to the refectory. I looked at the basket, and I saw it contained fifteen or twenty rolls at the most. Don Bosco carried out the distribution with a smile and a word of greeting to each boy. To my great surprise, I saw the same quantity remain in the basket which had been there from the start, though no other rolls had been brought and the basket had certainly not been changed. I was so impressed and excited that when my mother came shortly afterwards to take me home, I said to her: "I am not leaving this place, Mother. Don Bosco is a saint, and I want to stay with him."

Francis Dalmazzo became a Salesian and was the first rector of the Salesian Parish of the Sacred Heart in Rome.

"Take and Eat. . ."

A similar phenomenon occurred one morning at Mass in connection with the Eucharist. It was the Feast of Our Lady's Nativity, and about six hundred boys were present in church. The ciborium in the tabernacle was almost empty, containing at most twenty particles. The sexton had prepared another ciborium for consecration, but at the last moment forgot all about it and left it in the sacristy. At communion time, when Don Bosco uncovered the ciborium he had taken from the tabernacle and noticed its contents, a look of distress came over his face. The altar boys noticed that he raised his eyes to heaven in mute supplication and then went down to give communion to the first row. But one row succeeded another, and still there were hosts in the ciborium, and when all the boys had received—most of those present did—there were still as many particles as there were at the beginning.

Word spread quickly among the boys. "Miracle! Miracle! Don Bosco is a saint!" they were saying as they crowded around him after Mass. "Are you sure?" he kept repeating to them, and added: "When you think of it, boys, isn't the Eucharist always a miracle?"

Extraordinary happenings are many and varied in the life of Don Bosco: cures, conversions, foretelling the future, but he always played down the part he had in them. For him, they were simply a striking evidence of a person's trust in the Lord. Yet seldom did the people around him fail to note that, if the "miracle" was wonderful, no less wonderful was the faith of Don Bosco who, in difficult and often trying circumstances, could say with utter conviction: "God will help us!"

CHAPTER IX

THE FOUNDER

"The Lord and the Devil"

Don Bosco knew what he needed for the future of his Oratory: boys who would absorb his spirit and methods, and become hard workers and loyal helpers. There was no other way. Even the best among his priest friends, who for years had assisted him in his work, were not at all willing to live the rugged life of the Oratory for the rest of their days.

He had rather poor material with which to build. Most of the Oratory boys lacked even the rudiments of an elementary education. He kept his eyes open, and encouraged the most promising: Michael Rua, John Cagliero, Angelo Savio, John Francesia, and a few others. He directed them toward the priesthood; sent them to school to complete their secondary education, and, at a proper time, gave them cassocks. They lived at the Oratory; took part in the recreation where they unobtrusively supervised the games and taught catechism—young men, all of them; some only in their late teens.

"What a fine group of young men to build into a religious order, Don Bosco!" a visiting Capuchin missionary told him one day.

"Don Bosco, you are not going to live forever. What's going to happen to the Oratory after you die?" This from the Archbishop of Turin himself.

"What are you waiting for, Don Bosco? The time to start

71

your religious society is now! Don Cafasso had even been blunt about it.

But the decisive argument came from an unexpected source, Italy's Minister of Justice, Urbano Ratazzi who had been responsible for the anti-Church laws of the newly unified country, and who, for that reason, was often referred to as "that devil" by some outraged Catholics.

"You know how I feel about your work, Don Bosco," the lanky magistrate told him one day. "Every town in Italy should have an Oratory. I can't think of anything that could benefit this country more. You ought to choose a few priests and laymen and form them into a society with definite rules and regulations. You must impart your spirit into these people so they become not only your helpers but also your successors."

"Your Excellency," Don Bosco replied, "you actually promoted the suppression of religious orders in Italy. Are you suggesting that I start one?"

"I know the laws of suppression, Father. They create no obstacle because you could found a society which meets the conditions of the laws."

"But how could that be?"

"Your society should in no way reflect the condition of the old religious orders. It will be more like an association of free citizens who have united and live in common for a humanitarian purpose."

"Will Your Excellency give me the assurance that the government will permit the founding of such an order and will let it live?"

"Unquestionably, Father."

When Don Bosco related to his young assistants what

had transpired during his conversation with Ratazzi, impulsive John Cagliero remarked: "We are quite sure that Don Bosco's inspiration to found the Salesian Society comes from the Lord, but I never thought its greatest push would come from the 'devil.' "

Enter the Pope

The approval and the blessing of the Holy Father were essential to Don Bosco's plans. In March, 1858, accompanied by Michael Rua, he went to Rome and personally presented to Pope Pius IX a letter from the Archbishop of Turin detailing his work at the Oratory and his plans to form a religious society. It was Don Bosco's first meeting with the Pope, and the exchange between the two men could not have been more cordial.

"They tell me you keep yourself and a lot of people very busy in Turin," the Pope said, smiling.

"Your Holiness, my boys keep me busy all the time."

"What actually is the work you do at the Oratory?"

"Most anything, Holy Father. I say Mass, preach and confess, go begging, teach several hours a day, and occasionally even help with the work in the kitchen. . ."

In a succeeding audience, the Pope questioned him at length about his past and the origin of the Oratory. He insisted that Don Bosco set in writing all he had told him. "The Lord's designs are clearly manifest in your life," he said. 'These things should not be lost to those who will come after you, Don Bosco."

The Pope could not have been more favorable to the

ideas and plans Don Bosco submitted for his society. He made some very pertinent suggestions, and commended the rules Don Bosco had drafted, promising his support for the definitive approval.

Pius was quick to note the innovator in Don Bosco. Indeed, the ideas of the Turin priest were bold, if not revolutionary. His religious society was not meant to be just another religious order. His plan encompassed a program in which clerics and laymen would live and work side by side, totally committed to the Salesian ideal. He went even further, and cast his net wide. He was actually envisioning "Salesians in the world," both priests and laymen bound only by their common goal of spreading and implementing the message of the Gospel, with youth, neglected youth particularly, their first concern.

The Pope was amazed at the broad approach of Don Bosco's plan. He stressed, however, the importance of the vows and of community life. "Without vows," he said, "the unity, the spirit and even the work of the Society could not be permanently upheld." He did agree that the rule should be flexible and easy to observe, and the lifestyle of the Salesians—their garb and religious practices—such as not to attract the attention of the world.

While Don Bosco revised some of his original ideas in order to conform them to the guidelines established by the Holy See, he held to the concept of a religious society open to both clerics and laymen. "Coadjutors," he named the latter. Though they might outwardly appear as laymen, they were as fully religious as the clerical members, equal to them, in fact, in everything except the priestly character.

The Salesian Coadjutor is probably Don Bosco's most

genial creation. Not only the Salesian Society, but the entire Church was enriched by the dedicated lives of thousands of these "religious in secular clothes," humble and selfless men, many of whom became renowned in the industrial arts, contributing mightly to the Salesian educational program.

It was Easter, and for Don Bosco an added joy to be in Rome at such a time. As assistant to one of the officiating cardinals, he was privileged to be close to the Holy Father during the Holy Week services. He was in the papal procession when, after the solemn Mass on Easter Sunday, the Pope was carried to the great balcony overlooking Saint Peter's Square for the final blessing *Urbi et Orbi*. It was while on the balcony that Don Bosco, surrounded as he was by a great many dignitaries, found himself trapped between the papal chair and the massive stone railing of the balcony. His shoulder came up to the level of the portable platform supporting the chair on which the Pope sat. Suddenly he realized that the Pope's right foot was actually resting on his shoulder, a rather delightful if somewhat embarrassing situation that helped make that Roman Easter all the more memorable for him.

"I, a Monsignor? Oh, No!"

Before he left Rome, Don Bosco was once again received by the Pope, who greeted him with a smile. "Don Bosco," he said, "what in the world were you doing Sunday on the balcony, under my chair, acting as if you were needed to shore up the Vicar of Christ?" It was a most cordial audience that gave Don Bosco the opportunity to explain further his plans for the future of his work. Once more the Pope made several suggestions and promised his full support.

"One more thing, Don Bosco, before you leave. I should be pleased to make you a monsignor. . ."

Don Bosco's face dropped. "I, a monsignor? Oh, no, Your Holiness! Can you picture me all dressed in purple among those street urchins? They would run away from me. . .And would people still believe when I told them I was poor and needed money?. . .Thank you, Holy Father, but just let me be poor Don Bosco!"

The Pope stood up and gently placed his hand on Don Bosco's shoulder. "There is something I know you won't refuse," he said as he walked toward a safe. He opened it, took out several large gold coins and gave them to Don Bosco. "Be sure you give a treat to those youngsters," he said, "and bring them my blessing."

"What more could I expect?" Don Bosco whispered to Michael Rua as they left the audience hall. Young Rua was too moved even to speak. He just looked at Don Bosco. Never before had he seen such a glow of happiness on that fatherly face.

"Rome is Eternal"

It was a jubilant Don Bosco who returned to Turin. The new Society, even if not definitely approved, could now function. The draft of the rules was not yet final, but it was a working plan. He could now raise his banner. He could develop a spirit of unity and stability which would give permanence to his work.

"Rome is eternal in more ways than one," a Vatican Monsignor had told Don Bosco when he had attempted to draw him out on the time it would take for the formal approval of his society. It was not until March, 1869, that it was finally granted, and it was only in 1874 that the rules were officially approved.

"The task of founding a religious society in our times," Don Bosco later remarked, "was absolutely above human power. Had I foreseen all the obstacles and trials that stood in the way, I would never have had the courage to carry out the undertaking. What could poor Don Bosco have done had he not been visibly guided by the Lord and His Holy Mother? God is blessing our endeavor and His will is that we shall go on. . .Who knows but that He wills to make use of this humble Society to achieve great things in His Church? Who knows but that in twenty-five to thirty years' time, our little nucleus, with the Lord's blessing, will not go out into the world and become an army of over one thousand religious?"

Prophetic, but much too conservative, was Don Bosco's forecast. Less than a century after the definite approval of the Society, the professed members in Don Bosco's religious family numbered over forty thousand, their rate of growth being one of the fastest ever registered in the history of the Church.

CHAPTER X

COOPERATORS

"I Need You More Than I Need Money"

It was Carlo Buzzetti's first visit at the Oratory, in May, 1852. An architect, he had heard glowing reports about the place from boys he had met on his jobs and was anxious to meet Don Bosco, their hero. What he found was a large playground teeming with youngsters, most of them poorly dressed, engaged in all sorts of games, and, he thought, remarkably well-behaved. Suddenly, as if by magic, at the sound of a bell, all games came to a halt. The boys, still happily chattering, made their way to the two buildings at the far end of the courtyard.

It was sometime before Signor Buzzetti, with the ready assistance of one of the boys, was finally able to corner Don Bosco. "It's surprising what you have here, Father," he said after introducing himself. "I know some of your boys, and would like to be of help, if I may. I am in construction work and might be able to do something for you."

"You won't believe it," Don Bosco smiled warmly, "but what I really need right now is a few men like you. I could use you more than I could money. . .Do you have a few minutes? I'll show you what I mean."

It was a Saturday afternoon, and the boys were engaged in varied activities: band and choir practice, stage rehearsals, catechism classes, or just plain house chores. Don Bosco and his guest stopped by the window of one of the large classrooms on the ground floor. A medley of jarring sounds could be heard, typical of band instruments tuning up.

"You probably recognize their maestro," Don Bosco said. "He heads Turin's municipal band. He comes twice a week to instruct our boys. We would be lost without him." Under a shed, some twenty youngsters were watching intently while a man was explaining to them the intricacies of an hydraulic saw. "He is the manager of the sawmill across the river," Don Bosco pointed out. "He puts in quite a few hours of his free time to teach our boys."

They moved on to the makeshift chapel where a large group of boys stood in rapt attention, taking in every word from a short, round, jovial priest. "My good friend Father Borel," Don Bosco explained, "takes time from his seminary teaching to help me with the catechism classes. . ."

Don Bosco then led the way down the basement staircase. They were soon in a large room where a dozen women were busily mending piles of clothes. They greeted Don Bosco warmly, but kept right on with their work. "My mother, Signor Buzzetti," and the priest pointed to the elderly lady who was quite evidently in charge. Mama Margaret nodded and smiled, but she, too, went right on with her work.

They were back in the courtyard. "Now you see, Signor Buzzetti," Don Bosco said, "what I mean when I say that I could use a few men like you. In your line of work, you have carpenters who might be willing to give some of their time, or any skilled worker for that matter. . ."

"I will certainly look into that, Don Bosco. It's amazing what you are doing with these youngsters. My brother

Giuseppe will want to know about all this. You can count on us, Father!"

Who Should Thank Whom?

It was June 21, feast of St. Aloysius, one of those eventful occasions that made life at the Oratory a joy. Some five hundred boys from the nearby tenement houses joined the resident students for the solemn Mass in the morning after which lunch was served *al fresco*. And what a treat it was to delight those famished youngsters!

"Don Bosco, who's paying for all this food?" there was a note of dismay in Don Rua's voice.

"Don't you know? Signor Cotta and his wife. . ."

In the afternoon, at the solemn procession, Turin's most famous band, in full uniform, was in the lead, and its strains brought the people out on the streets by the hundreds.

"How in the world can Don Bosco afford this?" someone asked within hearing of one of the Saint's assistants.

"He can't," the young cleric replied. "General D'Agliano is paying for the band."

Later in the day, the boys had the time of their life on the green meadows surrounding the Oratory buildings: games of all kinds, gymnastics, races. . .Trophies and cash prizes were awarded to the winners and refreshments to all. As darkness fell, hundreds of Japanese lanterns turned the place into a fairyland, and the long-awaited fireworks brought the evening to a spectacular close.

Not a cent had come from Don Bosco's pocket to cover

the expenses of the feast. His friends had done it all: Signor Cotta, Count Cays, General D'Agliano, and Count Cavour. They had spent most of the day at the Oratory, enjoying the feast as much as the youngsters.

After night prayers under the stars, Don Bosco spoke briefly to the boys. "We have these gentlemen to thank for the wonderful day we have had," he told them, pointing to his smiling friends who stood by the platform from which he was speaking. The youngsters' rousing cheers and applause were heard blocks away in the silence of the night. But the Saint did not have the last word. "We are the ones who should thank you, Father," Count Cays said to him before they parted. "We had a marvelous time, and this is certainly not the only blessing we expect to receive from the little we did for you and for your boys."

Anything to Help Them

"We have a good many youngsters knocking at our door. We simply must expand or leave them out on the street." It was something Don Rua had heard from Don Bosco time and time again.

"But where is the money to come from this time?" Even Don Rua, his closest assistant, at times wondered if Don Bosco was not being reckless.

"A lottery, a nation-wide lottery," Don Bosco replied with a smile. "Let's form a committee." The roster of names on the committee read like Italy's *Who's Who*. Obtaining the license from the government was no trouble, since Italy's deputy premier headed the committee. Next, providing the lottery prizes: paintings, objects d'art, genuine oriental rugs, quality furniture, even carriages and teams of horses.

Don Bosco's friends went knocking at some of Piedmont's most aristocratic homes. No one could say no to Don Bosco. The prizes rolled in by wagonloads. The most valuable were exposed in the lobby of Turin's Art Museum, and all were listed in the newspapers all over Italy. The Oratory's presses were kept running round the clock, printing the tickets—thousands of them—while in nearly all of Italy's major cities, distributing committees were set up to peddle the tickets from door to door. Finally came the drawing day, a gala occasion at the Oratory, with recitals, choir and band selections interspersing the endless calling out of the winning tickets.

"Don Bosco has made more money than he can spend in ten years," some of his critics were heard to say. The truth was that most of it went into paying overdue debts, and the rest as a first payment on the much-needed expansion at the Oratory.

The gift of knowing how to make people work for a good cause was part of Don Bosco's genius. The lottery was not the only project that proved it. Those were the days when young apprentices were completely at the mercy of their employers. There were no laws, and certainly no unions to protect them from the abuses to which they were subjected. Don Bosco got his lay friends to sponsor his boys as apprentices in factories and shops. Contracts were drawn up that would assure a decent treatment for those boys. The men actually toured (often with Don Bosco) the places where the young employees were working to see that the employer lived up to the contract. One such contract, duly notarized, was recently found. In it a Turin jeweler (a Cooperator) vouches for one of Don Bosco's boys, a sixteen-year-old orphan, as an apprentice in a stained-glass studio. The employer, on his part, pledges himself to take the boy under his wing for three years, "to teach him the art without making him do other extraneous work, to let him free on Saturday afternoons and Sundays, and to give him fifteen days' paid vacation every year. Furthermore, the young man shall be paid two Liras weekly during the first year, the pay to be doubled on each of the two succeeding years." Labor unions should all vote Don Bosco their patron saint.

It was Don Bosco's way of implementing his words: "Anything and everything to help these youngsters."

In Union There is Strength

"Cooperators" Don Bosco called his lay friends who were willing to assist him in his work. He soon realized that some sort of organization was needed. He often said: "A number of willing, committed Christians, joined together by the same ideal, can generate an irresistible strength for good."

After evening classes one night, in 1850, he invited several of his lay assistants for a glass of Barbera wine. Between sips, he told them he had a mind to organize them into an association that would eventually expand outside the Oratory walls. It was a first attempt in the realization of a long-standing dream. When, in 1864, he presented Pope Pius IX with the first draft of the Rules of the Salesian

Society, the Pontiff, who was leafing through its pages, was struck by the heading of the last chapter: *The Society's External Members*.

"Who are they?" he asked.

"Your Holiness, please read on," Don Bosco answered.

The Pope did, with amazement. "Any person," the document stated, "living in the world with his family, may belong to our Society. Such a person need not take vows, but shall simply try to live up to the Society's rules, its spirit and program insofar as his age, condition and work will permit." It was a bold project, far in advance of the times, and Rome did not approve it.

Even among his own Salesians, Don Bosco at first made little headway when he spoke to them about the Cooperators' association. "A confraternity?" they asked. "There are too many prayer groups already!"

"You do not understand what I mean," Don Bosco replied one evening after another long discussion with some of his assistants. "I want no part of a confraternity or a third order that would limit itself to prayer and devotional practices. Our Cooperators are to be activists, involved in anything and everything that might help implement the message of the Gospel, especially where the young and the poor are concerned." And he added: "The times are past when all one needed to do was unite in prayer. Today the world wants action. The devil, too, has changed his tactics. We must beat him to the game!"

He moved to organize the Cooperators' association in 1875, and presented them with a constitution and a program of action which is as vast as the needs of the Church and society in general. This time the Pope approved his plan enthusiastically, and asked that his own name be placed on top of the list of the newly formed association. Within a short few years the Salesian Cooperators numbered two hundred thousand in Italy alone. Wherever the Salesians opened an establishment, they could count on a well organized group of Cooperators to assist them. For them Don Bosco founded the *Salesian Bulletin* which, for more than a century, has chronicled their mighty accomplishments and has inspired them to new conquests with the Founder's famous motto: Give me souls!

The message Don Bosco penned for his Cooperators shortly before he died is a masterpiece. "I have not had the joy of meeting most of you personally," he wrote in part, "but I know that someday we shall meet in a better world and shall rejoice over the good we were able to accomplish together. Let me just tell you this: Without you I could never have done anything. It was you who made it possible for the Salesians to bring help, comfort and joy to countless youngsters."

CHAPTER XI

A LIVING MONUMENT

"Something Is Missing"

It was a warm June night in 1864, and Don Bosco stood on the balcony overlooking the Oratory playground. The boys were at their games, and occasionally some of them would look up and wave, shouting a greeting to him. It had been a very busy day for Don Bosco. He was now relaxing and talking with Father Lemoyne, one of his assistants.

"Don Bosco," Father Lemoyne said, "don't you think something is still missing to complete the work of our Society;"

"What do you mean, Father Lemoyne?"

"You have done so much for boys; why not something for girls, too? Wouldn't it be wonderful if we had Sisters doing for girls what we are doing for boys?"

"Father Lemoyne," Don Bosco replied, "don't you suppose I have been thinking about that? I have even been having dreams about it..." He went on to say he had dreamt he was with Marchesa Barolo who, out of a clear sky, began to tell him that he should confine himself to boys, since her nuns were taking care of the girls and doing a good job at it, too.

"I told her quite simply that a priest's task was to take care of souls, all souls, and that included girls. The Marchesa retorted, 'Indeed, the Lord came to save all. You don't have to tell me that, Father, I know it. . .' You might just smile at that dream, Father Lemoyne; but, if anything, it means that I have been thinking of doing what you propose. Please God, we'll get to it soon."

On a White Horse

Late in the afternoon of a bright October day in 1864, a group of Oratory boys, some of them riding horses, arrived at the sleepy little village of Mornese on one of their famed excursions through the hills of Piedmont's picturesque Monferrato region. They had persuaded Don Bosco to mount a white horse, and the villages could hardly believe their eyes when the caravan, at the sound of drums, paraded through the narrow streets all the way to the parish church where they were overnight guests of the Pastor, Don Pestarino, a Salesian, who had invited them to eat some of the luscious and tasty grapes ready for the picking in the nearby vineyard.

But something more than a pleasure ride had decided Don Bosco to visit Mornese. He was anxious to meet a group of young women who, with Don Pestarino's blessing, had formed a sodality to assist in parish work.

"They are my angels," Don Pestarino had told Don Bosco. "They do wonders for the parish, teaching catechism to the youngsters, and conducting a sewing class for the girls. It's like a tiny oratory of their own. They want to meet you, Father. Who knows that this may not be the beginning of something even bigger!"

Maria Domenica Mazzarello was the sodality's prime mover. She led the way with the energy of a born leader and the unassuming gentleness of a mother. She was enchanted to know Don Bosco had finally come to Mornese, and directed her fellow sodalists to do whatever was needed to make his and the boys' stay at Mornese as pleasant as possible.

Don Bosco met the group on the following day, after Mass in the parish church. He encouraged them to continue their good work "because the Lord and Our Lady have great things in store for you. . ." Late that day, after the guests had left Mornese and everything had returned to normal in the village, Maria said to her friends, "I am now more than ever convinced that Don Bosco is a saint. . ."

"Stars Under Our Feet"

The tiny oratory at Mornese under Maria's watchful care was like a cenacle where ardent young souls were being trained for the greater things to come. Sewing was not the only reason why the Mornese mothers entrusted their daughters to Maria and her friends. "They are like Sisters," they used to say. "They know exactly what to do with our girls."

"Don't become just seamstresses," Maria would tell her eager pupils. "Become the very best of seamstresses!" When the hour bell struck, "One hour closer to heaven," she would say, "or don't you think about it?" And again, "Why not make with every stitch an act of love for the Lord?" Occasionally she accompanied them home after dark. "Look at all those stars," she would say. "One day, in heaven, we shall have them all under our feet. . ."

During the months that followed his first visit at Mornese, Don Bosco was in constant touch with Maria and her sodalists. They were, he knew, under Don Pestarino's excellent care. "In all that regards you," the latter told them, "I am Don Bosco's voice." One day he returned from Turin with exciting news. "So far," he told the young sodalists, "you have been staying with your families. Would you be willing to leave home and live together under the same roof? It is what Don Bosco would like you to do." Nearly all the sodalists agreed. Maria and her friends, with two little orphan girls, were soon housed in a solid but simple structure that had been built on Don Pestarino's own property.

"A Great Task Awaits You."

"You are now a community," Don Pestarino told the twenty-seven young women. "You must now have a superior. . ."

Maria Mazzarello was elected by a nearly unanimous vote. "Why me?. . ." she asked almost in tears. She begged to be excused from the position, and acceded only when Don Bosco insisted. Nothing changed in her life. She took her turn in the kitchen, at the wash tub, and in the vegetable garden with the same ease with which she taught catechism or embroidery.

Not every one at Mornese was happy to see those fine young peasant women turn into a community of nuns and live in the building which originally had been intended to house a school for boys. There were open hostilities which, in some instances, verged on persecution. Don Pestarino bore the brunt of the attacks while Maria and her "Sisters" suffered in silence. The storm eventually subsided and soon

Mornese knew what a treasure of a "family" was housed in the Pestarino building high up in the Borgo Alto section of the village.

On August 5, 1872, the Bishop of the Diocese blessed the religious habit for the new Sisters. Don Bosco came from Turin for the eventful occasion. He had already informed them that they were to be known as *Daughters of Mary Help of Christians.* "Your institute," he told them, "has come into existence because Our Lady willed it. You are to be a living monument to her goodness." When he spoke to them at the clothing ceremony, he referred to the hardships and tribulations they had sustained. "You have had your share of sufferings," he said. "But can followers of a Crucified Lord expect otherwise? There is a great task awaiting you, and the trials you go through are meant to strengthen and prepare you for that task. So take courage! You have a new religious garb; it is meant to mark you as persons consecrated to God. Let your conduct prove you such. Let those who come in contact with you find you somewhat reserved, but always friendly. A Salesian Sister may at times have to lower her eyes, but she need never lower her head."

The handful of courageous young women became a legion. From Mornese they swarmed to every country in the world. In oratories, schools, hospitals, leper colonies, some twenty thousand Salesian Sisters—Daughters of Mary Help of Christians—work with the same spirit and devotion which at Mornese marked the life and work of humble Maria, now Saint Maria Domenica Mazzarello.

CHAPTER XII

GO INTO THE WHOLE WORLD

They Dropped Their Spears

One night Don Bosco dreamt he was standing alone on what appeared to be a vast treeless plain, extending as far as the eye could see. Suddenly there appeared on the horizon a horde of savages, very tall, long-haired and dressed in animal skins. They were shouting and prodding with their spears several missionaries in varied religious garb whom they felled and slaughtered one by one. Don Bosco was horrified.

"Will it ever be possible to tame those savages?" he was asking himself when he noticed that a new group of missionaries was approaching from the opposite side with a number of boys walking in front of them. He was amazed to recognize in them his own Salesians. Distressed, he was about to shout to them to turn back when something incredible happened. The savages first looked at the boys, then at the missionaries, and immediately dropped their spears and came forward to meet them as if they had always been the best of friends. Soon they were all kneeling and singing together. . .

The dream left Don Bosco wondering. Was his newly-founded society to become involved in mission work? Where? Who were the tall savages he had seen in his dream? Were they from Australia, Asia, or the Americas? He consulted several books and even an anthropologist friend, but got nowhere.

93

Early in 1875, the Italian Consul in Argentina was visiting the Oratory. Don Bosco questioned him on his experiences in South America, and was amazed to find out from the Consul's description of the Pampas, and even more from his photographs of the natives, that the place of his dream was unquestionably the Patagonia region of Argentina. Nearly one hundred thousand Indians roamed the bleak Pampas, in the most abject condition and constantly harassed by the colonists and the government troops. Charles Darwin, who had visited a few years previously, described them as "the tallest, most athletic Indians in the Americas, the most backward and impervious to any civilizing effort. . ."

An inquiry at the Vatican's Propagation of the Faith Bureau revealed that the missionary endeavors among the natives of Patagonia and Tierra del Fuego had been extremely few and with disappointing results; often, too, with disastrous consequences. The Vatican informant wondered "if the Salesians might not consider sending missionaries to those regions."

"A Little Nothing. . ."

On November 11, 1875, ten Salesians, all volunteer missionaries to Patagonia, stood in the sanctuary of Our Lady's church for the farewell ceremony. The Turin newspapers had given front page coverage to the "new missionary venture"; and not only the church, but even the large square fronting it was filled with well-wishers.

Don Bosco spoke feelingly at the service. "It is only a

tiny stone," he said, "we Salesians bring to the building of God's Church. But who knows that this little nothing may not be the beginning of something that will grow beyond our fondest dreams. . ."

At the close of the ceremony, Don Bosco embraced each of the missionaries and then accompanied them to the carriages lined up in front of the church, ready to leave for the port of Genoa.

"Do you want the Lord's blessings to follow you?" he said to them. "Then look only for souls. . .The youngsters, the sick and the old should be your first concern."

Brave Men

The new missionaries made Buenos Aires their home base, and the Oratory they opened in the city soon rivaled Turin's in size and variety of activities.

In the meantime they planned a strategy for the "conquest" of Patagonia. They were brave and zealous men, but they soon realized that the task was far above the strength of ten men. Their appeals for help did not fall on deaf ears. So great was the enthusiasm generated by their letters to Turin, that Don Bosco was hard put to satisfy the requests of all who wanted to go to Argentina. To Father John Cagliero, who headed the mission, he wrote: "Were I to allow all who volunteer to join you, I would be left without a single Salesian in Turin."

Father Cagliero's plan was bold: open as many bases as possible among the white colonists who, incidentally, were themselves in great need of religious assistance, and then move on to contact the elusive Indians. But in the meantime the governments troops, harassed by the natives, were ready to spring an all out attack. The Salesians asked to become army chaplains, hoping thereby to lessen the impact of the conflict, and, if possible, to prevent it altogether.

"Brother!. . .Brother!. . ."

The bloodiest encounter took place in the winter of 1886. The missionaries had persuaded the troops to use peaceful tactics as far as possible, and never to attack the Indians unless threatened. However, the natives feigned friendship, but then let fly their poisoned arrows. In a few minutes over four hundred were cut down by the soldiers' deadly fire. From then on, whenever the Indians were spotted, the missionaries would approach them first, offering them presents and shouting "brother!. . .brother!. . ." in their language. They would thus persuade them to come to terms with the government troops. Their efforts not only proved successful, but won for the missionaries the lasting friendship of the suspicious and embattled Indians.

Within the span of four decades, mission centers dotted Patagonia and Tierra del Fuego. Villages with schools, churches, and clinics literally transformed the face of the Pampas. The white colonists, too, benefited immensely from the work of the missionaries. As for the Indians, when disease, the inevitable consequence of their contact with the whites, struck down those unconquerable sons of the wild, it was again in the Salesian missionaries that they found their most trusted friends and protectors. The limited material comforts the missionaries brought those vanishing tribes, and the peace and contentment many of them found in the Christian faith were no small solace as they moved irrevocably toward near total extinction.

Since 1875, some ten thousand Salesian missionaries have followed in the footsteps of the ten men who first blazed the missionary trail for the youthful Salesian Society. They have gone everywhere in the world, the words of Don Bosco echoing in their hearts: "Look only for souls."

CHAPTER XIII

MAN FOR ALL SEASONS

"It's Not That Hard"

"Don Bosco, you have flooded Italy with your pamphlets. I saw your *Catholic Readings* everywhere. How do you do it? Where do you find the time to write?"

Don Bargotti, editor of Italy's foremost Catholic paper, wanted to know. He had come to the Oratory to interview Don Bosco, and was out to get the facts.

Don Bosco smiled at the ebullient young editor. "Father," he replied, "it's not that hard! I burn the midnight oil, as you yourself must do. That's it."

It is what Don Bosco did right to the end of his life. He devoured books (the Oratory's library was one of Turin's best), and wrote with ease on a variety of subjects. Some seventy books came from his pen, ranging from a brief treatise on the metric system to a full-length, well-researched *History of Italy*, probably his finest literary work. Unbeknown to him, this book was translated into English and published in London, in 1881, by Longman & Green Publishing Company. In the preface, after asserting that "writing a complete history of Italy is an arduous task indeed," the translator, I.D. Morrell, LL.D., former Inspector of Her Majesty's schools, writes:

"The book was originally written for Italy's secondary schools by Giovanni Bosco, a scholarly Italian priest. It has had a most remarkable success, having had several printings.

In translating this work I have essayed to adhere to its very attractive if simple style. . ."

When indeed did Don Bosco find time to write? Stealing it from his sleep, obviously; but in other ways as well. There were the rare times when he would leave the Oratory and spend the day at the home of friends, buried in his work. On the train, he would invariably place his bag on his knees, pull out rolls of galley proofs and go right on with his work oblivious of all the noisy and often strange goings-on in the third class coach.

His was a plain, simple, extremely readable style. He learned soon enough to shed the bombastic rhetoric, typical of the times, which he had picked up in school. He would often read what he wrote to Mama Margaret whose unerring instinct for simple phrasing was easily jolted by high-sounding words or long-winded sentences. "You lost me," she would say to John while listening, intent on her sewing. And John was quick to blue-pencil the abstruse word or phrase.

He kept the Oratory printing and bookbinding shops humming away, and nothing would please him more than when his boys came up with a brand-new copy of his latest work. "Here is your book, Father," they would say to him, glowing with pride. "No," he would reply, "not my book, our book. You worked as hard to print it as I did to write it."

"Had he wanted, Don Bosco could have made a name for himself as a writer, a name to stand among the best of his time. But his life was meant to be spent in works of charity for the young. He bent his uncommon genius for writing to that end. Although he did not live to produce a great literary masterpiece, he left the impress of a great mind and a great heart in writings that have done souls unimaginable good." These are the words of Pope Pius XI who knew Don Bosco personally, and lived to bestow on him the grestest of all honors: sainthood.

"Don Bosco Will See It Through"

There was more than a tinge of bitterness in the Pope's voice as he addressed the assembled cardinals on a subject "very close to our heart." Plans for erection in Rome of a great basilica in honor of the Sacred Heart of Jesus were floundering. The foundation of the new church was barely above ground when work had come to a halt for lack of funds.

"What has happened to all the promises of financial support that came from wealthy Romans?" Pope Leo XIII asked. "A fast-growing section of Rome," he continued, "is being deprived of a much-needed place of worship. And what of the sorry spectacle this unfinished church presents to the world?"

"Your Holiness, put Don Bosco in charge," suggested Cardinal Alimonda. "He will see it through to the end."

"But will Don Bosco accept?" asked Pope Leo eagerly. "The poor man has enough problems on his hands, feeding his youngsters. . ."

"Holy Father, for Don Bosco a wish of the Vicar of Christ is a command."

Don Bosco went to work. At sixty-seven, undaunted by failing health, he took on this heavy burden at a time when seemingly he had exhausted every known means of raising money for his own projects. "The Pope wants it," he said to his worried assistants. "It is for the good of souls, and it will give us Salesians a foothold in Rome. I told the Holy Father that the one condition I place to this undertaking is that an oratory and a school be included in the plans. He was delighted."

He approached the new task with his usual energy and sagacity. He wrote a circular letter to the episcopate of the whole world and to the editors of Catholic periodicals, explaining the nature and object of the undertaking. He persuaded wealthy Catholics to finance specific items, such as the massive granite columns of the church, the altars, the pulpit, the organ, etc. Leo XIII, who had informed him that he could do little to help him, came generously to his assistance. Still, money was needed all the time, and it did not always arrive in sufficient quantity to prevent the suspension of work. It was then that he thought of France.

"Father," the French Salesians warned him, "French Catholics are being drained for the bulding of their own Basilica to the Sacred Heart at Montmartre in Paris. How can you expect them to give to your church?"

"How little you know your own country!" he replied. "France is a great country, with money for every need. Say what you like, but despite storms and trials, she remains to those who know her well, and I am one of them, generous France!"

France gave Don Bosco a triumphal reception. It was as if he had been known, loved and expected wherever he went. Wrote *Le Univers*, Paris' prestigious daily:

"For the past week, religious circles in Paris have talked

of nothing but Don Bosco and his Oratory. The Italian St. Vincent de Paul is now spending a few days in Paris. . . Long lines of carriages are seen standing in front of all the places he visits. Members of the aristocracy vie with one another to have him as their guest, and crowds of people fill the churches he goes to."

At the Madeleine, Paris' most fashionable church, the crowd was so large Don Bosco had difficulty reaching the pulpit. His French was faltering, his delivery low-toned; yet his listeners, though accustomed to the best French pulpit oratory, were deeply impressed. He spoke of the young, especially the poor and neglected among them, and what they meant to the future of the Church and of society in general. The new Church of the Sacred Heart in Rome, he told them, was to provide a care center for such youths. And couldn't Paris, too, use one such center?

"These youngsters need you," he added. "Quite simply their salvation is in your pocket. Either we set them on the right path now, or they will one day become a threat to society, to us—you and me."

France was generous to Don Bosco, and put into his hands over one hundred thousand francs. Friends and contacts were made, too, that would prove very helpful for years to come. Part of the money went to the church for which he was responsible in Rome; part, to meet some of his most pressing debts; and the balance was used for the new Salesian Center which two years later was established in Paris.

"Was That Man Victor Hugo?"

Monsieur Boullay could hardly believe his eyes. "Tell me," he asked his friend Father Roussel, "was that bearded old gentleman I saw you with by the gate Victor Hugo?"

"Yes, but, please not a word about it! He came secretly to speak to Don Bosco, and I wouldn't want anyone to know."

"So the old agnostic, too, felt the pull of the saint, eh, Father?" Boullay went on. "What do you suppose the two talked about?"

"That, I don't know. But come in, M. Boullay, Don Bosco is waiting for you."

Boullay's visit with Don Bosco was most cordial. A distinguished Paris lawyer, he wanted a special blessing for himself, his two young daughters, who were with him, and his ailing wife. "Don Bosco," he said when he was about to leave, "I see you had quite a visitor a few minutes ago. . ."

"Who told you?"

"Your host, Father Roussel."

"Yes, it was Victor Hugo. He is old, and I did my best to turn his thoughts to God. We must pray for him. . ."

Why would the great French writer want to visit Don Bosco? Victor Hugo was then eighty-two years old, still shattered by the recent death of Jules Drouent, his beloved life-long friend and companion. He must have felt that a visit to the Turin priest, about whose presence in Paris the newspapers were filled, could bring him a measure of comfort. In his memoirs, Don Bosco details the long dialogue between himself and the famed author of *Les Misérables*. That Victor Hugo must have been impressed is clearly testified by his parting words to Don Bosco. "Monsieur l'Abbe, I trust you will continue to be my friend. In spite of what I might have told you during our conversation, I do believe in God, and hope that, when my time comes, a priest will be at my side to assist me."

When two years later Victor Hugo lay dying, the Archbishop of Paris was informed that the renowned Frenchman had asked to see a priest. Unable to go himself because of illness, the Prelate sent one of his priests to the Hugo residence. The priest was kept waiting in the servants' quarters for more than two hours and was finally told that Victor Hugo had died and there was no point in seeing him.

"So they did not let you in to see him," the Archbishop said to the priest. "I knew his friends would do something like that. France's greatest self-professed agnostic making his peace with God? They would never allow a thing like that! It is most unfortunate, but don't feel too bad, Father. You were not by Victor Hugo's bedside when he died, but I am sure the Lord was."

"Why Doesn't He Leave Me Alone?"

Don Bosco came in late for lunch on a cold November day in 1854. He held in one hand several letters intended for the mail. After greeting his young assistants he told them, "I have got letters here going to some very distinguished people: the Pope, King Victor Emmanuel II, and the hangman."

There was a burst of laughter among his listeners who wondered why Don Bosco would associate the name of hangman with the revered names of his other two correspondents.

"It is not at all a laughing matter," Don Bosco continued, explaining that the young son of the hangman was so ostracized in the Turin public school that his father had asked that the boy be admitted to the Oratory. As for the letter to the Pope, he was not at the moment in a position to reveal its contents. "What about the one to the King?" someone asked. "It contains a grave warning for His Majesty," Don Bosco replied.

He then went on to tell them that for days he had been haunted by a strange dream. "It seemed to me," he said, "that the door of my room suddenly opened wide. A court attendant in full uniform stood there looking sorrowful and grave. "There are to be solemn funerals at Court!" he shouted. He closed the door and left. A dream is a dream, and one should not give it too much importance. But I feel the King should be warned. As you know he is about to sign into law the confiscation of a great many church properties. Who knows? He might decide to give the matter more thought."

It was not the first time Don Bosco had warned the young King. It pained him to see him at the behest of anti-Church politicians who, in the name of a unified Italy, were seeking to undermine the Church at every step. After one such warning, Victor Emmanuel was heard to exclaim: "I love Don Bosco; I even help support his boys. Why doesn't he leave me alone?"

In January, 1855, less than two months after Don Bosco's prediction, the mother, the wife, and the brother of the King died, all of them after a brief illness, only days apart from one another. Since Don Bosco's message to the King had become known, the impression in Turin was enormous. Through the troubled years that followed, eventually leading to the unification of Italy with Rome as the capital of the new kingdom, Don Bosco quietly continued his behind-the-scene work, often at the request of the Pope, to smooth out the differences between Italy's government and the Vatican. The King, too, appreciated his efforts.

Speaking one day to Marquis Fassati, one of his close attendants, Victor Emmanuel asked him: "Tell me about Don Bosco. You know him better than I."

"I might tell Your Majesty that he is a saint. But that, Your Majesty knows already," replied the Marquis. "This much I'd like to say: Few men are as devoted to the Church as Don Bosco; few as loyal to Your Majesty."

"You've said it all quite well! Thank you, Marquis," the King replied.

"We Never Heard Such Sermons Before!"

On his first visit to Rome, in 1858, late one evening, while Don Bosco was resting after a particularly busy day, Don Rua knocked gently at his door.

"An unexpected visitor, Don Bosco," he said. "The private secretary of the Holy Father is here to see you on an important matter."

It was but a few days after Don Bosco's first audience with Pope Pius IX. What could this visit possibly mean?

"Your Reverence," the suave Monsignor said, "you must forgive me for coming at such a late hour. It is the Holy

Father's wish that you conduct the annual retreat at the women's detention house here in Rome. Would you accept?"

"How could I possibly refuse, Monsignor?"

It was a spur-of-the-moment decision by the Pope, who had been much impressed with Don Bosco and who felt he would be the ideal man for the difficult task. When, on the following day, Don Bosco reported to the prison to make arrangements with the chaplain, "When does the Retreat begin?" he asked.

"Today, Father. In fact, the inmates are already in the chapel, waiting for you."

Unperturbed, Don Bosco collected himself briefly in prayer and went to the pulpit for the first of several sermons he preached during the five-day retreat. Preaching four times a day was only part of his work. The prison chaplain later related that all of the 260 woman prisoners insisted on going to confession to Don Bosco. "We never heard such sermons before," he added. "It was unquestion-ably the most successful retreat in the more than fifteen years of my chaplaincy at the detention house."

"Don Bosco," continued the chaplain, "kept those unfortunate women spellbound with his preaching. He was particularly effective when he preached on sin. Toward the end of the sermon, he pointed to the crucifix. 'With all he did for us,' he said, 'will we ever want to offend him again?' Stifled sobs were heard all over the chapel. 'No, no. . . ' He then turned to the crucifix again, 'Lord Jesus,' he said, 'you have heard them. These dear souls are truly repentant. They do love you, Lord; and if they did wrong, it was only because they did not know what they were doing.' "No," concluded the elderly chaplain, "never before had I heard such effective preaching."

The Pope, too, made some comments when he was told of the great success of the retreat. "I had a feeling," he said, "that there is to Don Bosco a great deal more than appears at first sight. Now I know he is truly a man of God."

"Did I Really Say That?"

Despite his heavy schedule of work at the Oratory, Don Bosco seldom turned down an invitation to preach. He was certainly not going to refuse his old friend Don Clivio, pastor of Montemagno, a small agricultural center not far from Turin. Early in August, 1864, the priest had written to him, "Come, John, we need you at Montemagno."

The feast of Our Lady's Assumption, on August 15, was the town's great annual festival, preceded by three days of preaching and devotional practices. But those hard-working farmers were in no mood for celebrating. A frightful drought was threatening to destroy their crops. A few more days of blistering sun, and all would be lost.

"How about it, my friends," Don Bosco told his sparse audience toward the end of his sermon on the first day. "Let's put a lot of faith in what we do during these days, and, if need be, amend our ways with a good confession. Let's do it; and I promise you we'll have rain on the 15th, without fail."

"Some nerve, Don Bosco! How could you promise a thing like that, and with such assurance?" the pastor asked him after the sermon.

"What thing, Don Clivio?"

"The rain on the 15th-without fail. . ."

"Did I really say that?"

"You most certainly did! Ask anyone, John."

"Impossible! You misunderstood me. . ."

"Then a lot of us did, Father. . ."

On the two following days the church was filled to capacity at the evening service. The people took Don Bosco at his word. Don Clivio had to call on neighboring priests to help with the confessions. On the 15th, the day dawned as bright and hot as ever. The church was filled at all the Masses. "Everybody at Montemagno went to Communion, as on Easter Sunday," Don Clivio said later.

The church was again filled to overflowing for the Vespers service at 4:00 p.m. Still no rain. "Will it come?" people kept asking one another. "What if we get no rain, Don Bosco?" someone said to him in the sacristy as he was about to mount the pulpit for his final sermon. But Don Bosco hardly heard him, deep as he was in thought and prayer.

All eyes were fixed on him as he began to preach. He had said but a few words, when the sunlight streaming through the stained-glass windows seemed to dim somewhat. And then, suddenly, the first rumble of thunder. A murmur of joy ran through the vast throng. The sky was getting increasingly dark. Don Bosco's voice broke a few times as he tried to raise it amidst louder thunder claps. Finally the rain, pouring and beating against the windows.

There were muffled cheers; many people had tears in their eyes. Don Bosco, deeply moved, stopped preaching for a while, as the rain kept pounding on the roof and against the windows, and the thunder rumbled above. He finally resumed his preaching which ended in a hymn of thanksgiving to the Lord and his holy mother.

In the sacristy, after the sermon, Don Clivio embraced Don Bosco and said, "I told you the other day that you had a lot of courage. No, not courage, John: faith!"

CHAPTER XIV

IN HIS FOOTSTEPS

"Come Next Sunday"

Eight-year old Michael Rua was impressed. "Where did you get that nice tie?" he asked an older friend at school.

"I won it at a raffle at Don Bosco's Oratory," came the reply.

"Who is Don Bosco?"

"Oh, he is a fine priest who gets boys together on Sundays, teaches them catechism, and then plays all kinds of games with them."

"Can anybody join the Oratory?"

"You are a bit young, but come next Sunday anyway, and I'll take you to see Don Bosco."

For Michael, who had lost his father a few days before, meeting Don Bosco was a thrilling experience. "He is like Dad," he told his mother. A third-grade pupil at the Christian Brothers' School, he saw Don Bosco only occasionally, but grew more and more fond of him each time they met.

"Won't you give me a medal, too, Father?" he asked him one day, seeing he was distributing tiny religious medals to a group of boys.

"Here is the medal, Michael, And something else, too." Don Bosco replied. "The two of us some day will go half-and-half in everything. Here, let's begin right now," and with his right hand Don Bosco made a gesture as if he were trying to cut something on the palm of his left hand. "Come on, Michael, take your half." But there was nothing to take, and Michael wondered what Don Bosco meant.

Years later, when he became Don Bosco's right-hand man and shared with him the heavy responsibility of governing a growing Salesian Society, Michael Rua understood the meaning of Don Bosco's baffling words and gesture. In Don Rua, Don Bosco had a perfect lieutenant. "Why, if Don Rua wanted, he could even work miracles," he said one day with a smile.

"Is it really so Don Rua?" someone asked him.

"Don't believe it," he replied. "One day, Don Bosco asked me to take his place and go to bless a very sick woman. Well, I went, I blessed her and she died. . ."

"Make yourself loved," Don Bosco would occasionally say to his vicar, in an effort to smooth out his apparent air of severity. "Let me tell you a dream I had last night," the Founder said one day when, surrounded by his Salesians, he noticed Don Rua approaching the group. "I dreamt I was in the sacristy and wanted to go to confession. I was looking around for a priest and caught site of Don Rua saying his breviary. He looked so stern that my courage failed. I could not bring myself to go to confession to him, for fear he might be too strict with me." They all laughed heartily, Don Rua even more than the rest of them. But he took Don Bosco seriously, too. He worked with might and main to achieve in himself the fatherliness he so admired in Don Bosco till it was said of him that in this, as in everything else, Don Rua was a faithful replica of the Founder.

Don Bosco considered him a gift from the Lord. It was

this frail-looking man's uncommon energy, his unquestioned loyalty to the Founder, his deep spirituality, and his genius for administration that made him not only Don Bosco's greatest collaborator, but the obvious choice as his successor as head of the Society. Shortly before Don Bosco died, when the conversation veered to what some described as an uneasy future for the Salesians, Don Bosco remarked: "I do not think we need worry. We have men of high caliber in the Society. Take Don Rua for one. If the Lord were to say to me, 'Your time has come; choose your successor and ask me to endow him with all the gifts and graces you deem necessary,' I would not know what grace to ask for him. He is already blessed with them all."

"Michael, the two of us will go halves in everything," Don Bosco had told the little boy with a thin, pale face and round bright eyes. They did, literally, sharing work, responsibilities, problems, joys and sorrows—even the honors of the altar; for he is no longer just plain Michael Rua, but *Blessed* Michael Rua.

"Who is This Boy?"

For years, in a village church in Piedmont, Italy; under the portrait of a bright-faced adolescent, people read the following inscription and marveled that a mere boy of fifteen could have lived and died like a saint:

> *DOMINIC SAVIO – 1842-1857 – He wanted*
> *to do great things for God and souls; he wanted*
> *to be a priest. He was cut off in the flower of*

his boyhood and, through his lovable holiness,
has become a model for the youth of all times.

The Church declared Dominic a saint, the only teenager ever to be raised to sainthood who had not died a martyr's death. It has been said of him that he is the finest product of Don Bosco's educational system. Don Bosco himself tells us how he first came to meet him.

"It was," he writes, "the summer of 1854 when Mondonio's pastor came to see me about admitting a young boy from his parish to the Oratory. 'I doubt, Father,' he told me, 'if you will ever again meet the likes of Dominic in goodness and intelligence.' We agreed I would meet Dominic at Murialdo in the fall when visiting there with my boys.

"I must say I was quite impressed with Dominic when I met him. He was then a little over thirteen. We talked at length about his studies and his life at Mondonio. I then said to him: 'Dominic, I see you want to come to the Oratory to take up a Latin course. What is it you are aiming to become?' "

" 'A priest, Father, God willing,' he replied eagerly.

" 'I'll be happy to have you come, Dominic,' I replied. His face brightened, 'Oh, thank you, Father; thank you very much! I know you'll never regret taking me with you.' "

Dominic spent barely two years at the Oratory, but they might have been fifty if one is to judge from the lasting impressions he left there. That he was mature beyond his years is shown by the extraordinary influence he exerted on his companions, many of whom were a good deal older than he. "You have many fine boys here, John," Mama Margaret remarked to Don Bosco one day, "but none quite like Dominic Savio."

A born leader, he organized a group of the Oratory's best students into a society which had a unique stabilizing influence at the Oratory for years to come. Its aim was to help create in the school an atmosphere of healthy activity and cheerfulness which would assure a fine spirit and a high level of morality among the students.

But something deeper lay behind the large pensive eyes of this teenager, something that seemed to betray a communion with the Unseen, a communion that was soon to reach unexpected heights. Dominic knew his time was short. He astounded Don Bosco one day. "Father," he said, "I just feel I must become a saint—and soon. . .But I really don't know what to do. Saints did great things, all kinds of penances. You won't let me do any penance."

"Dominic," Don Bosco replied, "we become saints just by putting a lot of love and care in all we do, and doing it all with a smile, for the Lord, even when the going is hard. Will you remember this?"

"I will, Father!"

There were things about Dominic that not even Don Bosco could explain. One day the boy went to him, looking frightfully concerned. "Father," he said, 'I just have to go home. Mother is not well."

"But Dominic, we haven't heard anything of the sort from home. . ."

"Please, Father, I must go. It will only be a short visit."

He made it by carriage to Mondonio in little more than half an hour, and was walking home when he met his father running in the opposite direction.

"Dominic, why are you here? Who told you about Mother?"

"I just knew, Dad. Where are you going?"

"I am going for the doctor. Come with me."

"No, Dad, I am going to see Mother."

Mrs. Savio was expecting a child and having a difficult time. Dominic, oblivious of all that was going on in the house, dashed to her room. "Mother," he said, embracing her, "take this. . ." He took off his medal and chain and placed it around her neck. "I know you will be fine now, Mom," he assured her. He then kissed her goodbye and rushed off to catch the coach for Turin.

"Another time," relates Don Bosco, "he came to my room. 'Quick, Father, come with me,' he said.

" 'Where to, Dominic?' "

" 'Hurry, please, Father. . .' "

"I followed him as he led me down several streets without uttering a word. Finally, entering a doorway, he took me to a third-floor apartment where he briskly clanged the bell at the door. 'They need you here,' he said and left.

"A woman opened the door. 'It's my husband, Father. Come quickly or it will be too late.' The man had left the Church and was anxious to make his peace with God. He was barely in time to receive the last rites.

"Later I asked Dominic how he had known about the dying man. Embarrassed, he just looked at me while tears welled in his eyes. I did not press the point any further."

Dominic's health, never too strong, began to fall perceptibly toward the end of the winter, 1857. Don Bosco had a team of doctors examine him. They were amazed at his cheerfulness, his ready wit, and maturity of mind. "What a jewel of a boy!" one of the doctors remarked. They knew nothing could be done to stay the onslaught of his lung disease. Dominic knew it, too, and prepared to welcome death as a schoolboy might look forward to the happiest of holidays.

On the doctors' advice and somewhat unwillingly, Dominic went home to his parents. Shortly afterwards he took a turn for the worst. He asked for the Sacraments which, in the words of his pastor, he received "like an angel." On the evening of March 9, 1857, he suddenly called his father, "Good-bye, Dad," he said to him. "Good-bye! Oh, if you only saw what I now see!..."

"He was smiling," his father related. "It was the most beautiful smile I ever saw on his face. Then suddenly he was dead."

When Pope Pius XII canonized Dominic, in 1954, he said: "At the school of Don Bosco young Savio learned that one can become a saint simply by serving the Lord joyfully and making Him loved by others." It was Don Bosco's way and Dominic proved him right.

"I'll Donate Him to You."

His father was dead and he was becoming too much for his mother, a positive terror of a boy who was forever in trouble. Don Bosco met him one day while visiting Castelnuovo. He was struck by the twelve-year old's liveliness and mischievous smile.

"You are John Cagliero, aren't you?"

"Yes, Father. I think you know my mother..."

"I do, of course. Let's go to see her, John."

Young John's mother was a close friend of Mama

Margaret. "I wish your John, Don Bosco I mean, would take my boy off my hands," she had said to her once. "I can't manage him anymore."

"Teresa, I hear you want to sell me your son," Don Bosco said with a smile as he entered the Cagliero home with John.

"Father, I thought you knew that we don't sell boys at Castelnuovo. We sell only calves and chickens. . .If you want him, I'll donate him to you."

For John Cagliero Turin was an adventure, and the Oratory the answer to his dreams: sports, music, excursions, everything he had ever wanted. It took some time before he realized that all was not play; but when he did, he soon topped his companions with the exception of Michael Rua. He had a fierce sense of loyalty to Don Bosco. "I owe him everything I have," he said one day, "even the shirt on my back." Yet, when the moment came to decide whether or not he should become a Salesian, Cagliero wavered.

"He wants to make monks of all of us," someone whispered to him one evening after a conference with Don Bosco.

"You have a point," Cagliero replied. "It doesn't make sense to become a religious when religious orders are on the way out. . ." He thought about it for some time. The interior conflict did not last long. "How can I even think of leaving Don Bosco? Monk or no monk, I am staying with him."

Ordained a priest after he had received his doctorate in theology, he soon became proficient in music, too, and initiated a music program which brought great renown to the Oratory. His musical productions were an instant success, and his tuneful arias sung or whistled all over Turin. His composition *Il Figlio dell'Esule* (The Son of the Exile), when performed at Turin's Royal Theater, was given a standing ovation. Many thought they had listened to one of Verdi's latest productions.

Cagliero's incredible energy found full scope when, in 1875, he enthusiastically accepted Don Bosco's invitation to head the first Salesian missionary expedition to Argentina. His exploits are numbered among the great missionary achievements in the annals of the Church. In 1877, he returned for a brief visit to Italy to recruit personnel for his missions. One evening, after accompanying Don Bosco to his room, he was about to leave him when, "One minute, John," Don Bosco said, as he opened his desk drawer. . . "Take this. You will need it someday." Later, on opening the tiny box, Father Cagliero could not believe his eyes: a bishop's ring! "Someday. . ."

That day dawned on December 5, 1884, when he was consecrated a bishop and given episcopal jurisdiction over nearly all of Argentina's mission territories. In the evening of that eventful day for the Oratory, the new bishop, pointing to his ring, "Do you remember, Father? But how could you possibly know?"

"I knew it," Don Bosco replied, "a few months after you arrived as a boy at the Oratory. Do you recall how close you came to dying when you contracted typhoid fever during the great epidemic? For a while, I, too, thought it was the end of you. I came to your room to give you the last rites; and, suddenly, like a vision, it was all there before me. A dazzling white dove with an olive branch in its beak hovering over your pillow, while all around your bed strange men, savages actually, were bending over you, looking terribly concerned as if fearing you might die. It all lasted but a few seconds. I knew then you would live and become a missionary (the savages around your bed were a clear sign of that), and eventually a bishop, too, since that was the significance of the white dove with the olive branch. But dreams or no dreams," Don Bosco concluded, "here you are now, John: His Excellency, Bishop Cagliero!"

Bishop Cagliero continued his mission work for nearly thirty years, criss-crossing the South American Continent numberless times with the same vigor and enthusiasm he had displayed at the Oratory in the early years of his priesthood. Recalled to Rome in 1917 by Pope Benedict XV, he was created a cardinal, the first Salesian to attain the honor of the purple. He was often heard to repeat: "I once said that I owed Don Bosco everything, even the shirt on my back. But I never thought that I would live to be able to say that I owed him the cardinal's hat!"

The Tall Young Prince

"Royal" is the word that could best describe the reception Don Bosco was given on May 18, 1883, at the Lambert Palace while he was visiting Paris. Hostess of the gala event was Princess Marguerite d'Orleans, sister of Louis Philippe, Count of Paris, and wife of Polish Prince Ladislaus Czartoryski.

The day-long reception opened with the Mass offered by Don Bosco in the palace chapel. Prince Czartoryski reserved for himself and his 25-year-old son, Prince Augustus, the privilege of serving Don Bosco's Mass.

"I have been wanting to meet you for quite some time, Augustus," Don Bosco said to the tall young prince while vesting for Mass. The young man was known in the courts of Europe as much for his brilliant mind as for his intense piety. His mother, Princess Maria Amparo, was the daughter of Maria Cristina, queen of Spain. Prince Ladislaus Czartoryski had married Princess Maria in 1856, and Augustus was born in 1858. The child's mother died soon after, and Prince Ladislaus married Countess Marie d'Orleans from whom he had two other sons. As the first-born of Prince Ladislaus, pretender to the Polish throne, Augustus was in direct line of succession.

During the reception at the Lambert Palace, Prince Augustus was constantly at Don Bosco's side, "conquered," as he related later, "by the simple, gracious manners of that saintly man." Shortly afterwards, he visited the Oratory. "It was then," he told his friend Noguier de Malijay, later a Salesian, "that I discovered my purpose in life." That visit marked the Prince's first step in the long and painful journey that eventually brought him into the Salesian Society.

"My father," he told his friend Noguier, "thinks mine is just a passing fancy. I am dead serious about my vocation. I have no other interest in life and am quite prepared to renounce all my rights as the first-born son in the Czartoryski family. Ever since I met Don Bosco, I know I must be, and will be, a Salesian."

When it became clear that Prince Augustus was determined to pursue his vocation, his father tried to dissuade him from joining Don Bosco's religious family. "I know Don Bosco, and I revere him as a saint," he told his son, "but the Salesians are almost unknown. Besides, your frail health will never be able to withstand their rugged life. "Why don't you become a Jesuit?" Don Bosco kept prudently in the background. "What matters," he wrote to Augustus, "is that you do the Lord's will."

Undaunted and anxious to convince his father and Don Bosco, too, that his decision was God-inspired, Prince Augustus personally brought his case to Pope Leo XIII. "Go to Turin, my son," the pontiff told him after listening to him at length, "and tell Don Bosco to admit you into his society."

But the last battle had yet to be fought. Two days before the ceremony at which Augustus was to be given the religious habit, Prince Ladislaus, accompanied by his wife and Augustus' two step-brothers, arrived in Turin. A dramatic encounter took place at the Oratory. Tearfully, they pleaded with Augustus to reconsider his step. It was all to no avail, and the solemn ceremony took place in the Church of Mary Help of Christians on November 24, 1887, before an overflow congregation. Don Bosco gave the Salesian habit to Augustus, his friend Noguier de Malijay, and two other candidates, while the members of the young Prince's family looked on, resigned to "lose" their beloved Augustus.

Don Augusto, as he was familiarly known in the Society, was one of those rare souls destined by God for a very special mission: to inspire men to follow the magnificent example of total detachment and humility set by him during his short life. Ordained a priest in 1892, he died a little more than a year later, offering his young life to God with a prayer on his lips that the Salesian Society be enriched with many good vocations. It was a prayer which did not remain unanswered. From Poland, Don Augusto's native land, hundreds of young men flocked to enroll in the Society, among them the future second Salesian Cardinal, August Hlond.

The cause for the beatification and canonization of Father Augustus Czartoryski is well advanced in Rome. The proud family that had "lost" a prince gained a saint.

"Think About It, Philip!"

Young Philip Rinaldi folded the letter he had just read, and, looking up to his mother, "Why is Don Bosco so insistent?" he asked. "I told him so many times that the priesthood is not for me. Nothing will ever change that."

Insistent, Don Bosco had been ever since he had met Philip at the Mirabello Salesian School some eight years before. "Philip," he had told him, "What if the Lord wanted you to be a priest? Think about it." The fact was that the more Philip thought about the priesthood, the less he liked the idea. He felt he had made it clear to Don Bosco time and again. He had done so recently again with a letter in which he had informed him that he did not think he was fit for the priesthood, and that, in any case, his eyesight was poor and studying caused him intense headaches. And here now was another letter from him, more insistent than ever. "Come Philip," it read, "I promise you that your headaches will pass and that you will have enough eyesight to carry you through the priesthood and through life." In a postscript, Don Bosco was asking him to meet him at the Salesian school in nearby Borgo San Martino where he expected to spend the day on the following Sunday.

"I will go to see him, of course," Philip told his mother,

"but just to make it clear once and for all that I am not about to change my mind."

Sunday, November 4, 1887, was Founder's Day at the Borgo San Martino School. Hundreds of people had converged on the place to see Don Bosco. The bishop of the diocese, dignitaries and clergymen from the entire countryside had been invited. Philip could hardly hope to see much of Don Bosco on a day when everybody seemed to crowd around him whenever and wherever he appeared. But, as he was to recount later, the unbelievable happened. Don Bosco spotted him in the crowd and invited him to dinner with the guests of honor. Later, when everyone had left the dining room, the Saint motioned to Philip to stay for the talk they were both equally eager to have.

There is nothing in Philip's memoirs concerning this interview, but the outcome is itself revealing. Less than a week later, Philip was at the preparatory seminary. What he saw as he sat alone with Don Bosco in the community dining room on that bright November day must have impressed him even more than what he heard. Shortly before he died, he spoke about it, in a sworn testimony, to Don Bosco's biographer.

"Toward the end of the interview, Don Bosco, who had suddenly become silent, seemed to compose himself in prayer. He sat motionless, his head bowed, his hands crossed over his chest. Soon his face began to radiate a light which gradually became brighter, brighter even than the sunlight that streamed through the windows. After a few brief moments, he became his normal self again, resumed the conversation, and, rising to his feet, begged to be excused and headed for the door."

Don Bosco's exceptional interest in Philip's career continued unabated even after the young man joined the Society. No sooner had Philip been ordained a priest than he appointed him rector of the seminary for delayed vocations. Surprisingly, he even invited him to attend the monthly meetings of the Superior Council, the highest governing body of the Society. It was an unheard-of privilege for a young priest, still relatively unknown among the older Salesians. One day, on one of his private visits to the Founder, Philip found him pouring over a map of the world, spread open on his desk.

"Would you permit me to go to the missions, Father?" Philip asked him.

"Philip," he replied, "you will stay here to send others to the missions." He then pointed to Australia and remarked that the Salesians would go there someday. "And you will be the one to send them there, Philip," he added. Then pointing to Spain, "Here is your field of action," he told him, and went on to speak of frightful reverses for that Catholic country during which much blood would be shed, "Salesian blood, too, And you will live to see it all, Philip."

It all began to happen after Don Bosco's death. Following several years of fruitful work in Spain, Father Rinaldi was recalled to Turin by Don Rua and appointed to the second highest post in the Society. Elected Superior General in 1922, he headed Don Bosco's religious family during its greatest period of expansion, and presided over the beatification of the beloved Founder.

"There was something charismatic about Father Rinaldi's insight into the mind, methods and spirit of St. John Bosco. That he joined dynamic action to a profound understanding of Don Bosco's mission is his great merit, and the reason, too, behind the results that crowned his work as Superior General of the Salesian Society." These words appeared in the *Osservatore Romano,* the Vatican official newspaper, when notice was given that the cause for the beatification and canonization of Father Rinaldi had been introduced.

Shortly before he died on December 5, 1931, Father Rinaldi wrote; "As I draw near the end of my life, I can see more clearly than ever how bright was the light that led me to our Blessed Founder." He must have found, too, at that point the answer to the question which, as a reluctant young man, he had asked himself so often, "Why does Don Bosco insist that I become a priest?"

CHAPTER XV

THE WAYS OF A SAINT

"Invariably Cheerful"

"At first sight, you might have thought of him as just a good, simple country priest, with a pleasant smile and bright, penetrating eyes; but start talking to him, and suddenly you were mesmerized." It was the way Father Michael Fassio put it when asked what Don Bosco was like.

"He was invariably cheerful," Father Fassio continued, "full of fun, really, to the very end of his life. I remember one day when he visited our home on the outskirts of Turin. He was then close to seventy, and looked even older than his age. Once he sat at table with us, he seemed to find his old energy and sparkle again. His conversation was spirited and full of humor. He had us all laughing so much with his pleasant jokes and tricks that we almost forgot to eat. I recall that we were served walnuts at the end of the meal. With the simplest of ease and joking about it, he kept cracking one nut after another by squeezing it between his thumb and forefinger. 'It's easy,' he kept telling us. . .'Try it. . .' None of us, not even the older ones among us, could do it."

"Don Bosco, how on earth do you keep all those enterprises of yours going?" a successful businessman once asked him.

"I go on like a steam engine, pouf. . .pouf. . ." he replied.

"Yes, but how do you keep the engine going?"

"Mostly I trust in the Lord. Right now I so trust He will inspire you to help my boys that I am quite certain you'll do it."

His trust in Divine Providence at times took on unexpected forms. To a wealthy widow, who asked him how best she could invest her fortune, "Put it right here, Madam," he replied, opening both hands.

"I won't let you go," implored another lady, "until you have given me your autograph." On a piece of paper, he wrote: "Received from Mrs. Bianchi the sum of two thousand liras for my boys. Signed, John Bosco," and offered it to her with a smile.

The Right Approach

It happened at Marseilles, at the home of a wealthy benefactor who had invited Don Bosco to be his guest of honor at a formal dinner. A lady friend of the family, who was anxious to see the priest everyone called a "saint," entered the dining room toward the end of the meal to find Don Bosco standing with a glass of champagne in his hand, toasting his hosts and doing it with great humor to the delight of all present.

"He, a saint?" the lady thought to herself. "Saints don't go around drinking and cracking jokes. . ."

A few minutes later, while she was standing with other

guests in the foyer, Don Bosco came by on his way out. He suddenly stopped, and turning to her, "Madame," he said gently, "do you remember the words of St. Paul: 'Whether you eat or drink, or whatever you do, do it all for the glory of God.'?"

"Oh, Father, won't you, please, forgive me?" It was all she could say as Don Bosco smiled and moved on.

At a reception given in his honor, among the guests was an old retired general, known for his anticlerical ideas. The general was much impressed with Don Bosco, but did not get up enough courage to speak to him. The guests were beginning to leave when he finally approached Don Bosco. "Father," he said, "at least a parting word from you. . ."

"General," Don Bosco replied gently, "you took part in many a battle. There is one more you can't afford to lose. . . ."

"Which battle, Father?"

"The one that will see you safely home," Don Bosco answered, pointing toward heaven.

The general replied, deeply moved: "I know what you mean, Father. . .I know what you mean. I promise to do something about it, too. . . ."

When travelling by coach, Don Bosco usually managed to get a seat beside the coachman. He would chat with him pleasantly on all sorts of subjects, and gradually lead the conversation to more serious things.

It was shortly after Easter. He was seated alongside the driver on the way to Castelnuovo, and the two fell to talking about the unusually warm weather they were having. "The warmest Easter I ever recall," the coachman remarked.

"By the way, my good man," Don Bosco asked, "did you make your Easter duty?"

"No," he replied. "Frankly, it's been years since I have been to confession. But, on my word, if I could find the priest to whom I made my confession some years back, I'd go immediately."

"Who was he?"

"Don Bosco, 'the boys' priest.' Perhaps you have heard of him. . ."

Don Bosco laughed. "You have found him. I am Don Bosco. . . ."

The man stared. "Why of course. I never did recognize you, Father. But I can't very well make my confession now, can I?"

"Why not? Give me the reins. . . ." And while the horses trotted on, the driver poured out his soul to the priest.

"A Poor Priest Like Me"

"Brother, I know you take care of Don Bosco's room. See that these two shirts get to him as soon as possible." The lady placed the neat package in Brother Peter Enria's hands, and vanished before he could even say a word of thanks.

Don Bosco was not in his room, and Brother Peter left the package, partly opened, on his bed. He noticed that the shirts were handmade and of excellent material.

"Peter, whose shirts are these?" Don Bosco asked him on the following day.

"Yours, Father. A lady brought them yesterday."

"A poor priest like me with shirts fit for a king? Oh, no. . ."

"What shall I do with them, Father?"

"Anything you want, Peter. Keep them for yourself, or sell them, or give them to somebody. . .I won't be seen wearing those shirts, Brother!"

It hurt him to spend money on himself. Before leaving for Rome in 1858, he went to visit a friend. The cassock he was wearing, while spotless, was patched in several places.

"You are not going to Rome with that cassock, are you Father?" his friend asked him.

"Why not? It's the best we have in the house. Actually, it's not even mine. I borrowed it from one of the Fathers."

One day, walking with Don Bosco on their way to visit a benefactor, Don Rua noticed that his shoes, rather old and worn, were not tied with laces, but with twine blackened in ink.

"Don Bosco, look at your shoes. How can you? Let me go buy a pair of shoelaces."

"If you really must," he replied, "here is a dime."

A barefoot beggar was suddenly standing there with an outstretched hand.

"Michael, give me back that dime. Talk about shoelaces! This poor soul does not even have shoes. . . ." He gave the dime to the beggar.

"How About It, Carlo?"

He went to a barber shop one day where he met a young apprentice with whom he was soon conversing.

"Your name?"

"Carlo Gastini, Father."

"How old are you, Carlo?"

"Fourteen. My father is dead, and I must help support my three younger brothers. . . ."

"How about it, Carlo? Suppose you give me a shave?"

"Oh, no!" interjected the shop owner. "I hired him only last week. He couldn't even shave a dog. . . ."

"Well, he's got to learn sometime. Come on, Carlo!"

During the painful half-hour that followed, Don Bosco kept calmly talking to the boy about the Oratory, its boys, games, and feasts, occasionally coaching him on the rough spots of the shaving operation.

"Not bad, is it?" he said to the owner as he got out of the chair, patting his chin.

"He half-flayed you, Father," the man replied. "Give him a tip if you want, but you won't have to pay for the shave. I should be paying you!. . ."

"Carlo," Don Bosco called to the boy, "a little more practice and you'll be a first-class Figaro! Here is your lira. See you Sunday at the Oratory?"

"I Don't Want to Lose My Baby."

"Don Bosco is not well, Mrs. Ceria. He cannot possibly see you. I will tell him you came. He will pray for you and send you his blessing." Much as he tried, Father Viglietti, Don Bosco's secretary, could not convince the young expectant mother, who stood before him in tears, pleading to see Don Bosco.

"I came up two flights of stairs just to see him, Father. I want him to bless me and the baby I carry. Please, Father, I lost two of them already!"

"All right, Mrs. Ceria. Wait here. Please, sit down and stop crying."

"Oh, thank you, Father!. . . ."

A few minutes later, the door to Don Bosco's room opened, and the good Father stood there smiling, an old blanket around his shoulders.

"Oh, it's you, Mrs. Ceria," he said. "You came all the way up here just to receive this poor man's blessing. You deserve a big one; yes, you do!"

"Don Bosco, I don't deserve it; I need it, more for my baby than for myself. . . .Oh, Father, I don't want to lose this one. . . ."

"You won't, Mrs. Ceria. Here, now, you don't have to kneel. And I want you to smile. You'll have a lovely baby, one that will give you much joy. Bless yourself now. . ." Don Bosco traced the sign of the cross on the woman after invoking for her Our Lady's intercession.

"Stop worrying now," he reassured her. "Here, let me see you out."

"No, Father, please. . .I know my way. You don't have to trouble yourself. You are not well. I'll take it easy on the way down."

Supporting her by the arm, Don Bosco accompanied her down the two flights of steps, gently warning her to step slowly and to hold on to the banister with her hand.

"Oh, Father, how can I ever thank you? The way I feel, I know everything will be fine. . . ."

"And you'll be back with your baby to thank Our Lady. . . ."

"Of course, I will, and to thank you, too, Father."

The birth of a healthy baby boy shortly afterwards was only the first of many reasons that brought joy to Mrs. Ceria. She lived not only to have several other children, but the "child of Don Bosco's blessing," as she used to call Eugenio, became a Salesian priest and the esteemed author of eight large volumes of Don Bosco's biographical memoirs.

"With the Charity of Christ"

No attacks against the Church were more bitter than those that came from the pen of Louis De Sanctis, a former priest, who had joined the Waldensians. With his monthly *Catholic Readings,* Don Bosco sought to offset the harm done by the ex-priest. While De Sanctis' writings were often offensive and even scurrilous, Don Bosco's rebuttals, though firm and direct, were inspired by a true Christlike charity.

In November, 1854, De Sanctis fell into disgrace with the Waldensians and had nowhere to turn. Hearing of his plight, Don Bosco wrote to him. Only a Christlike heart could dictate such a letter.

"I have been thinking of writing to you for sometime if only to tell you that I would be very pleased to offer you whatever a good friend can give. May I, therefore, invite you to come to see me at whatever time you may wish?

I shall gladly place a room at your disposal and welcome you to partake of our modest meals.

"You might say, 'What shall I do at the Oratory?' Whatever the Lord will inspire you, my good friend. You will be able to devote yourself to your studies. You need fear no expense. You will see that my feelings of friendship for you come from my heart."

"You can scarcely imagine," replied De Sanctis, "the effect your friendly letter had on me. I would never have believed that my most persistent opponent was possessed of so much kindness. You extend your hand to me! You practice the Christian love about which so many pointedly preach. . . ." He signed himself, "With sincere respect, your servant and friend."

Don Bosco did not let the matter rest with a brief exchange of letters. The soul of a brother priest was at stake. Here was someone who needed a friend. The invitation to the Oratory was renewed. "Since you call me a friend," Don Bosco replied in part, "I should be glad to meet you personally. . . .Would you like me to visit you at your residence, or would you prefer to suggest a meeting place in the city? Or you might wish to come to the Oratory. It would give me the greatest pleasure if you would do me the honor of coming to my house. I believe we would both be very happy with the solution, and no sort of pressure would be brought to bear upon you."

The invitation was accepted. Louis De Sanctis became a frequent guest at the Oratory, where he was always sincerely welcomed. He became convinced of the error of his apostasy and sought to return to the Church, but his way was barred by his wife, whom he did not have the courage to leave.

Don Bosco, seeking to surmount the difficulty, offered to provide a life annuity for the woman, but before it could be arranged De Sanctis died of a sudden heart attack.

Brother Joseph's Adventures

"Brother Joseph, I should like you to come with me to Caselle. We only have a few minutes to catch the train. Suppose you run ahead to get the ticket?"

"First or second class coach, Don Bosco?'

"You know I always travel third-class. . . ."

Those were the days when European trains had third-class coaches, uncomfortable, crowded, but cheap. They made it just in time to board the train when one of the station's officials recognized Don Bosco.

"Don Bosco in a third class coach?"

"Only because there isn't a fourth class," Don Bosco replied.

"No, Father. This train will not leave until I see you and your friend seated comfortably in a first class coach. And no extra money, either!"

"Joseph," Don Bosco remarked when they were both happily seated in the luxury coach, "Joseph, do you remember the Lord's words in the Gospel. 'Do not seek the first place?' Had we gone to a second class coach, we would probably have been left there. As it is, here we are, traveling like kings!"

Brother Joseph was involved in another episode not less revealing of Don Bosco's personality. The young lay-brother doubled as choirmaster and as headwaiter in the faculty dining room. One evening, Don Bosco was late for supper, having spent long hours in the confessional. All that was left was a bowl of rice that had not as much as been warmed up. Brother Joseph went to the kitchen and remonstrated with the cook, who was about to close up for the day.

"It's for Don Bosco. . . .Don't you have anything better?"

"Don Bosco is no better than anybody else," the cook shot back within Don Bosco's hearing.

Brother Joseph apologized to the Founder for the cook's irate remark. Without batting an eye, and trying to swallow the cold mushy rice, Don Bosco said quietly: "He is right. I have no business to be late."

A few days later, Brother Joseph was himself in trouble. Important guests had come for dinner, and everything went wrong with the service, beginning with a soiled table-cloth—"a positive disgrace," Don Bosco said later, speaking to the headwaiter. "You are in charge of the dining room, Brother Joseph," Don Bosco added, "how can you be so incredibly slipshod about things?"

Don Bosco's unusual outburst surprised and unsettled Brother Joseph. Later in the day he slipped a note under Don Bosco's door in which he told him he had never thought he could be treated so harshly by him. "I did not think it possible you could become so angry with anyone, least of all with me," the distraught Brother wrote.

On the following day, Don Bosco humbly apologized to Brother Joseph. "Do you remember, Brother," he told him, "what the cook said the other night about Don Bosco not being better than anybody else? Well, now you know it is true. I should try to be a whole lot better. You must help me with your prayers."

Some fifty years later, in 1929, when Don Bosco was raised to the honors of the altar, Brother Joseph Dogliani, then close to ninety, and a world-known and highly esteemed composer, recounting this and other episodes, exclaimed with tears in his eyes: "That was Don Bosco! No wonder he is a saint!"

"An Ugly Fellow"

Early in 1862, Don Bosco's close associates noticed that for several days their beloved Father, much paler than usual, seemed on the brink of exhaustion. One day, in the presence of several Salesians, "We are worried about you, Don Bosco," Father Cagliero said to him. "You don't look well. Is anything wrong?"

"I need rest," he replied. "I haven't had a decent night's sleep in a week."

"Father, do you have to work till the small hours of the morning? Try to get more sleep."

"I want to sleep, but someone makes me stay awake against my will," he answered. They clamored for an explanation. "You may not care or like to believe it," Don Bosco went on, "but the truth is that an ugly fellow is giving me a bad time." And he told them of loud noises, of gusts of wind that scattered his papers all over the room, and of sudden bursts of flames in the most unlikely places. "The moment I put out the lamp and try to go to sleep, things begin to happen, usually with the covers being violently pulled away from me. One night a horrible-looking monster pushed the door open and advanced toward me with open jaws. It disappeared at the sign of the cross, but the ugly fool manages to find its way back in one manner or another."

Father Angelo Savio volunteered one evening to stand watch in the foyer leading to Don Bosco's bedroom. He became so frightened at the horrible noises that he fled to his own room in terror.

The nightly attacks continued intermittently for some-time. Asked whether he was afraid of the devil, Don Bosco replied: "Being, as I hope, a friend of the Lord, I have no fear, since I do not believe he can really harm me. The old fiend thinks he can have the best of me and wear me out so as to stop doing God's work, but he has a long way to go." Asked whether there was a remedy to such infernal perse-cutions, he replied: "The sign of the cross and holy water offer some temporary relief. But I have found a way that is quite effective." When pressed to say more about it, he turned the conversation to another subject.

Noting that he would occasionally skip his meals or reduce them to practically nothing, some of his Salesians became convinced that the remedy to which Don Bosco alluded was the one suggested by the Lord Himself: "Certain devils are conquered only through fasting and prayer." (Matt. 17:21).

A New Brand of Diplomacy

Bettino Ricasoli, Italy's prime minister, came to the conclusion that only Don Bosco could solve his problem. The relations between the government and the Vatican had reached an impasse. Unless the thorny question of the appointment of bishops to half of Italy's vacant dioceses was solved, the very fabric of the government's relationship with the Vatican would come apart.

Ricasoli knew that Don Bosco enjoyed the full confidence of Pope Pius IX, that he was well thought of by King Victor Emmanuel II, and that he was, too, a saintly man. Who knows, the prime minister mused, but that where diplomats have failed, a saint might succeed. He sent for the Turin priest, who agreed to meet the prime minister at the Pitti Palace in Florence, on December 12, 1876.

Don Bosco, who had reasons to suspect that Ricasoli wanted him to play his game, astounded the prime minister at the very onset of their conversation.

"Your Excellency," he said, "I should like to remind you that I am a priest, not just at the altar and in the confessional, or with my boys in Turin, but a priest right here in Florence, and in this office."

"If I understand you correctly, Father," the prime minister replied, "you seem to imply that any term that might conflict with your loyalty to the Church would simply not be negotiable."

"What I mean," Don Bosco explained, "is that I can hardly be expected to bring to the Holy Father anything like an ultimatum from the Italian Government. What precisely does your government want?"

"The suppression of a number of bishoprics in Italy as a first step toward the appointment of bishops to the more important dioceses," said Ricasoli.

"Your Excellency, I would not as much as dare to suggest such a thing to the Holy Father. In practice, what you suggest is a weakening of the Church in Italy by suppressing a number of dioceses which the government finds expendable. This is unjustifiable interference in the affairs of the Church, against both the Italo-French Convention and the Italian Constitution. You should know that, Your Excellency."

The prime minister excused himself and left briefly to consult with the other ministers who were meeting in a nearby office. He returned to reassure Don Bosco that the question of the suppression of bishoprics was to be dropped. "We shall be grateful to you, Father," continued Ricasoli, "if you will assure the Holy Father on this point. He might then wish to proceed with the matter of appointing bishops to the vacant sees. . . ."

Later, the prime minister admitted to friends that he had been much impressed with Don Bosco's directness and firmness. "I realized that saints have their own brand of diplomacy, quite different from ours, but often more effective."

A Painful Calvary

"The heaviest cross I had to carry during my life was laid on my shoulders by the man I once considered my best friend." Don Bosco, who spoke these words shortly before he died, did not elaborate on them. The few persons to whom he had addressed them hardly needed an explanation. They remembered only too well the painful Calvary the beloved Founder went through for a decade, between 1873 and 1883, at the hands of Lorenzo Gastaldi, Archbishop of

Turin.

Lorenzo Gastaldi and Don Bosco were of the same age, and, when they first met as young priests, shared the same enthusiastic dreams of apostolate among the young. They became fast friends; and though Lorenzo, a brilliant intellectual, pursued his studies in search of all kinds of degrees, he was one of Don Bosco's most trusted helpers during the early, troubled years of the Turin Oratory.

So close were the two priests that, when Gastaldi left Turin for England on a special mission, he told his disconsolate mother: "My friend Don Bosco will take my place and be like a son to you." Recalled to Italy, he was appointed bishop of Saluzzo. Shortly afterwards, Pius IX, acceding to Don Bosco's suggestion, named him archbishop of Turin.

It did not take Don Bosco long to realize that a complete change had come over his once-trusted friend. The new archbishop, as jealous of his rights as he was conscious of his authority, opposed Don Bosco's new religious society on the ground that he could not tolerate in his diocese clergymen who were not directly subject to him and trained in his seminary. Even though he was aware that the Salesians had been approved by the Holy See, he was determined to keep the new society under his thumb. He pursued his purpose relentlessly with letters to the Vatican, misrepresenting Don Bosco's ideas and conduct. He snubbed him publicly, and even suspended him for a period of time from hearing confession in the archdiocese of Turin.

On his part, Don Bosco, while defending the rights of his religious family, never engaged in the least recrimination, and preferred to suffer in silence. He wept one day when the Archbishop dismissed him from his residence with a few curt words, without as much as entering into the subject for which Don Bosco had for months pleaded for an audience. "Why? Why?" he exclaimed in anguish as he and his secretary left the Archbishop's house. He then essayed his own answer: "I thought that with him as archbishop of Turin, we Salesians would have a smooth sailing. Oh, my poor human calculations! How much better to trust in the Lord!"

The stubborn opposition of Archbishop Gastaldi to Don Bosco is indeed difficult to explain. When people broached the subject to Don Bosco, he would invariably repeat: "The good man is in poor health. . .He is constantly under pressure by some of the men around him. . .He does not seem to understand us Salesians. . . "'

One thing is clear; whatever the Archbishop's feelings about the dynamic young Salesian Society, he never for a moment doubted its Founder's holiness. On October 28, 1882, shortly before he died, he presided at the inaugural blessing of the new Church of St. John the Evangelist built by Don Bosco on one of Turin's finest boulevards. After the service, in the sacristy, he pointed to Don Bosco, whom he had all but ignored up to that moment, and said to his seminarians: "I want you, young men, to come to assist at Don Bosco's Mass tomorrow. Look at him well. . . .You are looking at a saint!"

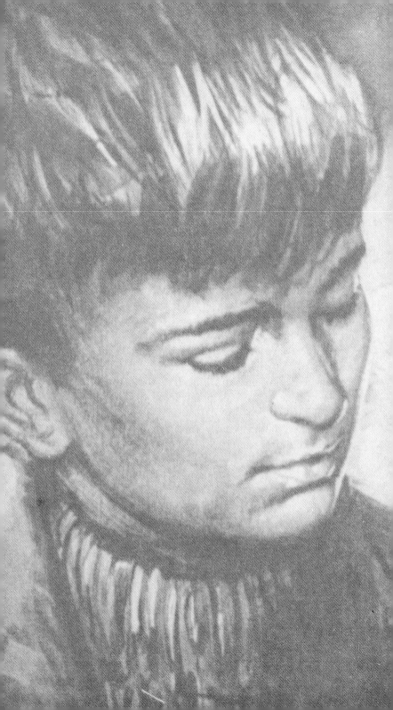

CHAPTER XVI

FAREWELL, FATHER!

"No Passport. . ."

When early in 1887 Pope Leo XIII was told that Rome's new Church of the Sacred Heart was to be inaugurated in May, he said: "I do hope Don Bosco will come to Rome for the occasion. After all, we owe it to him that the church was built."

"Your Holiness," his informant replied, "Don Bosco is far from well. It's doubtful if he can stand the journey. . ."

"Oh, but he must come," the Pope insisted. "Write to him that I expect to see him here in Rome. Tell him I won't give him the passport to heaven if he does not come."

In spite of the first class accommodations graciously provided by the Italian National Railroad, the journey was hard on Don Bosco. "How could I possibly refuse the Holy Father?" he told his jubilant Salesians and hundreds of friends who, on April 30, gathered to welcome him at Rome's Termini Station. He was given a triumphant reception at the new church, with formal speeches and brass band selections. At the end of the reception, he had them all laughing. "With all your fine speeches and kind expressions," he quipped, "you still haven't told me when we'll have dinner!" "But," related one of the Salesians, "even his ready smile and humorous sallies could not lessen the pain-

147

ful impression his stooping shoulders, labored breathing and tottering step made on all of us."

Those were incredibly busy days for Don Bosco. Endless lines of people waited patiently for hours for the privilege of a word with him or even just a blessing. The task of shielding him from the crowds became nearly impossible. "How the good Father can take all the turmoil around him without collapsing is a mystery," wrote one of the Salesians. "He is exhausted, and yet always has time for a good word, a smile and a blessing for everybody."

On May 11, Pope Leo sent word to him through his own personal secretary, Monsignor Macchi, that he would be "delighted" to see him on the 13th, the day before the dedication of the new Basilica. "The Holy Father will see you in the evening, Don Bosco," the Monsignor told him. "It is the time he always reserves for his closest friends."

The Pope received Don Bosco in his private study. Setting all protocol aside, Leo XIII helped him personally to an armchair near his desk. "It's a bit chilly tonight, Don Bosco," he said, "Here, let me put this coverlet on your knees. Isn't it beautiful? It's made of ermine, a gift someone has just made to me. Now, then, tell me how you are. . . "

"I am old, Your Holiness, and really not much good for anything anymore."

"But I am older than you, Don Bosco, and in no hurry to die yet. Don't you be in a rush, at least not until you hear that Leo XIII has died. . . ."

Don Bosco smiled. "Your Holiness, you may speak infallibly on certain things, and I wish I could believe what you have just told me. But I know I am at the end of my days. . . ."

The Pope wished to be informed in detail on everything that concerned the Salesian Society. He was pleased to hear that a great many young men were asking to become Salesians, and gave specific recommendations as to their training and formation. He was elated when informed of the progress of the Salesian missions. He then grasped Don Bosco's hands: "What about the future of the Church, Don Bosco?" he asked him. "Do you have anything to tell me?"

"I am no prophet, Holy Father, but if you insist. . ." He later related that he had told Leo XIII "what I knew," but never went into detail about the nature of the long conversation that followed.

Word that Don Bosco was at the Vatican spread quickly through the vast and silent halls of the great palace. Even though it was evening, the members of the Pope's official family came out to see the "Turin Saint. . . ." As he emerged into one of the hallways, a group of Swiss Guards presented arms in the traditional salute to dignitaries. Don Bosco stopped and, with his genial smile, said to them: "You needn't do that, my friends. I am just a poor priest, all hunched up and good-for-nothing." They lowered their halberds and, forming a circle around him, "Would you give us your blessing, Father?" one of them asked, while the others knelt or kissed his hand. Said one of the Salesians, who was present: "I wish that scene could have been photographed. . . ."

"Now I Understand."

The young Salesian who stood at the church's entrance directing the flow of visitors was approached by an elderly gentleman, who seemed unwilling to wait in line with the rest of the people.

"Is Don Bosco in the church?" he asked.

"No, not at this moment," the cleric replied.

"I am going home. . . ."

"Don't you want to see the new church?"

The man was a bit annoyed. "I did not come to see the church. I came to see Don Bosco. We have hundreds of fine churches in Rome, but where do we find a saint like him? Will he be here tomorrow?"

"Yes, he will. He will say Mass at 9:00."

"I'll be back tomorrow. . . ."

The man expressed the thinking of thousands of Romans who, on the weekend of May 14, flocked to the new Salesian Basilica not far from the Termini Station. Word spread that Don Bosco would offer Mass in the church on the following day. Even though it was fairly early and a weekday, the Basilica was filled to overflowing. Don Bosco offered Mass at a side altar dedicated to Mary Help of Christians. He was assisted by Father Viglietti, his personal secretary. Upwards of fifteen times during the Mass he paused, and was seen in tears. He was obviously very deeply moved.

Following the Mass, the people surged around him, as he slowly made his way to the sacristy. "It was a stampede," one of the Salesians related. "We shielded him the best we could from the more ardent enthusiasts, who sought to touch him and kiss his vestments. It was incredible! They could have forced their way into the sacristy if Don Bosco, barely able to stand anymore, had not turned to bless them just as the heavy sacristy doors were shut before the surging crowd."

In the sacristy, Father Viglietti, while helping him to take off his vestments, spoke gently to him. "Don Bosco, you did nothing but weep during the Mass. What happened?"

"My mind," he replied, "was constantly on the dream I had as a boy of nine. I was seeing it all over again: the majestic Man who bid me take charge of a crowd of neglected and unruly youngsters, telling me to treat them with kindness, and the resplendent Lady he gave me as 'your guide and helper. . .' Her words kept recurring in my mind, 'Johnny, someday, in due time, you will understand everything.' That was sixty-two years ago. Now I understand. . . ."

A Little Rest

Back in Turin, Don Bosco for the first time admitted he needed to rest a little. "I am beginning to think that doctor who examined me in Marseilles two years ago was right," he told Father Viglietti.

"What did he tell you, Father?"

"Nothing to cheer me up, really. He said I was like an old coat worn threadbare by too much use. No amount of patching will help anymore."

In July, he was persuaded to go to spend a few weeks at the Salesian School in Lanzo, at the foot of the Alps. The cool dry air would be easier on his lungs, and visitors would be less likely to disturb him. One day, in August, a large delegation representing the first Oratory boys came to see him.

Father Viglietti was adamant. "I thought the doctor made it clear that you were to have no visitors," he told him.

"Father Viglietti," he replied, "don't you know who those people are? I have known them for the last forty years. They are not visitors, they are my boys!. . ."

Shortly afterwards he presided over the annual retreat of his Salesians at the Valsalice Seminary, on the outskirts of Turin.

"You'll be back to visit with us again, won't you, Father?" the rector, Father Barberis, asked him as he was leaving for the Oratory.

"I'll do even better than that," he answered, "I'll be back to stay with you and watch over this place. . . ."

Father Barberis was puzzled. What did Don Bosco mean? They happened to be standing looking out over an outside flight of stairs which from the terrace led to the play-field below. "See that staircase," Don Bosco continued. "It will have to be remodeled. You'll be the one to get the plans ready."

To Father Barberis those words began to make sense when, after the Founder's death, the Valsalice Seminary was unexpectedly chosen as Don Bosco's burial place. The burial vault was built below that stairwell, and it was he, Father Barberis who, as rector, supervised the remodeling of the entire area which eventually was turned into a memorial chapel.

"Let's Go for a Ride."

December 16, 1887, was an unusually mild day; a pale sunshine bathed Turin's beautiful boulevards in a golden glow. "Don Bosco, let's go for a ride this afternoon," Father Viglietti suggested. "It will do you a world of good."

Don Rua went along with them in the sturdy old carriage of the Oratory. The two horses were going at a slow trot, and people, recognizing Don Bosco, greeted him enthusiastically along the way. "He was in great spirits," Don Rua related. "At a certain point he began to recite long passages from Latin and Italian poets, commenting on both their content and form."

Suddenly, on Victor Emmanuel Boulevard, they spotted the Cardinal-Archbishop of Turin, Cajetan Alimonda, walking with one of his priests under the arcades. Don Bosco directed the coachman to ease the carriage to the curb.

"Father Viglietti," he said, "go tell His Eminence that I would love to have a word with him. . . ."

The Cardinal rushed to the carriage, and embraced and kissed Don Bosco. "Don Giovanni, what a joy to see you! How are you? Of course, I'll be delighted to speak with you!. . ."

He sat by Don Bosco, while the people stopped to take in that rather unusual scene: Turin's two most celebrated churchmen in pleasant conversation right in their midst.

It was his last visit to the beloved city. "When he got back to the Oratory," relates Salesian Father Alfonso Volonte, a former student, "we were at our games in the playground. No sooner was the carriage spotted than all the five hundred of us boys rushed to greet him. It was bedlam, and I still wonder how the horses did not take a fit! In the midst of all the turmoil, all the good Father could do was wave his hands, his feeble voice drowned by our shouts. An armchair was waiting for him at the foot of the stairs. He was gently carried from the carriage and seated in the chair. Four of the bigger boys picked up the chair and carried him up the two flights of steps to his room. But we kept calling for him, looking up toward the balcony that fronted his rooms. He came out, supported by Don Rua and Father Viglietti. Again we let loose with our vivas until someone intoned what had become a sort of school song: 'Come, fellows, Don Bosco is calling.' He was trying to smile while waving to us, but we could see he was in tears."

"There Won't Be Any Jubilee."

Confined to his rooms, one of which had been turned into a tiny chapel, Don Bosco carried on much as usual, saying his Mass daily spending much of his time at his desk. He refused to turn away anyone who came to him, whether for confession, counsel, or even only for a blessing. He was always amiable and serene, often making light of his ailments.

"Don Rua," he once asked his vicar, "is there a place in Turin where they make bellows?"

"And what would you want bellows for, Don Bosco?"

"For my chest. . . ."

With his uncommon talent for rhyming, he would improvise little sonnets in Italian and Piedmontese, and then playfully recite them to entertain his visitors. "Come, listen to my latest literary production," he told a group of boys, who were visiting him. For several minutes he had them all laughing as he recited verse after verse of a sonnet with this refrain:

> O my poor legs now weak and bent,
> One day so straight and strong and fast;
> You'll never know how much I spent
> To keep you going and make you last.

Occasionally someone would bring up the subject of the golden jubilee of his ordination, in 1891. He would shake his head and say, pointing upwards, "Up there. . ." Countess Gabriella Corsi went to see him one day; she, too, turned the conversation to the jubilee.

"Don Bosco, I promised you I would pay for the banquet, no matter how many guests. I intend to keep my promise."

"You will not be able to keep it, my dear Contessa. And besides, there won't be any jubilee," he replied.

The elderly countess left, convinced that her own days were numbered. "I know what Don Bosco meant," she told Father Viglietti. "I must prepare myself." She died two weeks later.

Toward the end of December, he hobbled from his room to the infirmary to visit Father Louis Deppert who was "dying." "Louis," he told him, "you needn't worry about dying yet. Someone else will die in this bed first." Father Deppert recovered in a short few days; "miraculously," said the doctor. His bed was soon after transferred to Don Bosco's room to replace the rickety one he had used for some forty years.

One day, Don Bosco noticed that Father Viglietti, who was constantly at his side, was rearranging his clothes closet. "Would you do me a favor?" he asked him. "Go through the pockets of my clothes, and if you find any money, take it to Don Rua. People know we Salesians have no money in the bank or anywhere else. I want it to be known, too, that Don Bosco died without a cent in his pocket. . . ."

That the Salesians had no money was no fiction. On the very day on which the Founder died, the Oratory, with something like one thousand mouths to feed, was obliged, once again, to plead with the baker to bring the daily supply of bread on credit.

"It Is the Last Time."

They walked up the two flights of steps so quietly that Father Viglietti could hardly believe his eyes when he saw the boys, all fifty of them, members of the senior class, crowding the hallway in front of Don Bosco's room.

"You can't possibly see him," he told them. "He is much too sick!"

The boys would not leave. Reporting the unscheduled visit to Don Bosco, Father Viglietti said: "They may want you to hear their confession, Father. You just can't do it. . . You can hardly breathe. . . ."

"It's the last time. Let them come in," he replied in a whisper.

The doctor was not a bit pleased to see his patient expend his ebbing energies so recklessly. He ordered him to bed. Thereafter, only the Council's members and special visitors were admitted to his rooms. His priests vied with one another for the privilege of saying Mass in the little chapel adjoining the sickroom, happy to administer Communion to the beloved Father.

The presence of Bishop John Cagliero, his favorite missionary son, who had returned for a brief spell from Argentina, was a source of great comfort to him. He called him frequently to his bedside, sharing with him his final recommendations, as he did with his vicar Don Rua and the other members of the Council.

"Love one another," he told them, often with tears in his eyes. "See to it that a true family spirit prevails in our communities. . . .Work with faith, solely for the Lord and for the good of souls. If my faith had only been greater, how much more could have been done!. . .Love the Madonna," he told them one evening, as the bells of the nearby Church of Our Lady Help of Christians announced the Vesper service. "To her, we Salesians owe everything. . . ." Another time, seeing one of his young priests in tears at his bedside, "My greatest sacrifice," he said, "is that I must leave you." Asked what message he had for his boys, he replied in a whisper, "Tell them I will be waiting for them in heaven."

"Farewell, Father!"

After a little more than a month, during which hopes and fears followed in quick succession the ups-and-downs of their Father's illness, Salesians and youngsters alike knew Don Bosco was dying. The end came sooner than they had feared.

On January 30, 1888, word spread around the Oratory that the beloved Founder had lapsed into a coma, and that the doctors did not expect him to live through the night. The routine of the great institution came to a halt. All asked to see their Father one last time. "How could I possibly refuse them?" Don Rua said later.

First the priests, then the Brothers and the Sisters, and later all of the nearly eight hundred youngsters silently lined up in the corridors, on the stairways and under the arcades. Others came from the nearby schools and oratories; and as the word spread in the city, former pupils and friends joined the procession. They tiptoed through the room of the dying man. He lay motionless, his head slightly raised and inclined to the right, his eyes closed, his hands resting on the top of his covers. A crucifix had been laid on his breast; a violet stole, symbol of his priesthood, had been placed across the bed. They knelt briefly by the narrow bed, most of them in tears, and kissed the hand which had so often blessed them. The procession lasted far into the night.

At 4:30 in the morning, on January 31, 1888, as the Angelus bells rang from the church of his beloved Madonna, Don Bosco gave a gentle sigh and ceased to breathe.

* * *

EPILOGUE

"What was it that, during the past cold wintry days, brought some two hundred thousand people around the mortal remains of this humble priest?" The Turin daily which, somewhat rhetorically, asked this question in its editorial column the day after Don Bosco's funeral, did not attempt to give a reply. "Whatever it was," the editor wrote, "we were not at all surprised at what a Roman prelate, present at the funeral, told one of our reporters. Said the Vatican Monsignor: 'It was more than just a funeral. It was as if the people of Turin rose en masse to say to the world,' the Monsignor added, 'that the Church will eventually canonize Don Bosco. Turin did so today.' "

The editorial concluded: "Rightly, Don Bosco belongs to Turin in a very special way. Unquestionably, the Church some day will claim him among her saints. But we are certain that none of our readers, whatever their religious persuasion, will object if we say that, in a wider sense, Don Bosco truly belongs to the world."

*   *   *

On June 2, 1929, Pope Pius XI raised Don Bosco, whom he had known personally, to the honors of the altars, declaring him "Blessed." On Easter Sunday, April 1, 1934, the same Pontiff proclaimed him a "Saint" at what was then described as the most solemn canonization ever held in the Catholic Church.

* * *

"Tell me, Caterina," Margaret Bosco asked of her friend and neighbor Caterina Agagliati, "What do you make of my Johnny? What do you think he will be?" Signora Agagliati spoke with unusual solemnity this time. "Margaret," she said, "mark my word: that boy will have the whole world talking some day."

ABOUT THE AUTHOR

The family of Peter M. Rinaldi, distinguished for its service to the Church, had close contacts with St. John Bosco, the subject of MAN WITH A DREAM. Born near Turin, Italy, in 1910, Father Peter was the nephew of Father Philip Rinaldi, one of "Don Bosco's boys" and his successor as head, from 1922 to 1931, of the world-wide religious order founded by the Turin saint. In addition to his uncle, Father Peter knew other Salesians who were close to Don Bosco and whose names appear in the pages of this book.

Father Peter earned a graduate degree from Fordham University, held teaching and administrative positions in several Salesian schools, and was pastor of Corpus Christi Church, Port Chester, New York, from 1950 to 1977. An expert on the Holy Shroud, he wrote a great many books and articles about that relic, including *I Saw the Holy Shroud* and *It Is the Lord*. He also wrote *By Love Compelled*, a biography of his uncle, Father Philip Rinaldi, whom Pope John Paul II beatified in 1990.

Father Peter Rinaldi died in 1993.

OTHER BOOKS ABOUT SAINT JOHN BOSCO

Bosco, John. *Memoirs of the Oratory of Saint Francis de Sales*. The saint's autobiography up to 1855, with introduction, notes, illustrations, bibliography. 544 pp cloth $24.95

Desramaut, Francis. *Don Bosco and the Spiritual Life*. Study of his personal and educational spirituality. 348 pp paper $8.95

Lappin, Peter. *Stories of Don Bosco*. Popular biography for young adults (and older ones too). 264 pp paper $9.50

Pedrini, Arnaldo. *St. Francis de Sales: Don Bosco's Patron*. A study of the links between the two saints. 149 pp cloth $13.95, paper $8.95

Stella, Pietro. *Don Bosco: Religious Outlook and Spirituality*. Scholarly study of his thought and practice as writer, preacher, educator, spiritual guide, and founder. 616 pp cloth $49.00, paper $36.00

Stella, Pietro. *Don Bosco's Dreams: A Historico-documentary Analysis of Selected Dreams*. Foundational research into the nature, purpose, and types of his dreams, the insights into his personality and pastoral practice that they offer, and the value of the texts that relate them. 116 pp cloth $20.00, paper $10.00

Wirth, Morand. *Don Bosco and the Salesians*. Thorough treatment in popular style from 1815 to Vatican II. 432 pp paper $10.95

BOOKS RELATED TO DON BOSCO

Aubry, Joseph. *Savio: A Study Guide for Parents, Priests and Educators*. Accompanies Don Bosco's life of St. Dominic Savio. 69 pp paper $2.50

Bosco, John. *The Life of St. Dominic Savio*. The biography of one of Don Bosco's boys, written for teens and Christian educators; with notes and two appendices. 177 pp paper $8.00

Rinaldi, Peter M. *By Love Compelled*. The life of Blessed Philip Rinaldi, third successor of St. John Bosco as rector major of the Salesians. 215 pp + illustrations, paper $5.00